Speaking the Lower Frequencies

Speaking the Lower Frequencies

Students and Media Literacy

Walter R. Jacobs

STATE UNIVERSITY OF NEW YORK PRESS

Published by
State University of New York Press, Albany

For information, address State University of New York Press,
90 State Street, Suite 700, Albany, NY, 12207

Production by Kelli Williams
Marketing by Michael Campochiaro

Library of Congress Cataloging-in-Publication Data

Jacobs, Walter R., 1968–
  Speaking the lower frequencies: students and media literacy /
Walter R. Jacobs.
      p.   cm.
  Includes bibliographical references and index.
  ISBN 0-7914-6395-8 (alk. paper) – ISBN 0-7914-6396-6 (pbk.: alk. paper)
  1. Media literacy–United States. 2. Critical pedagogy–United States.
3. Mass media–Social aspects–United States. 4. Postmodernism and higher
education–United States. I. Title.
P96.M42U585 2005
202.3–dc22   2004048231

10 9 8 7 6 5 4 3 2 1

Contents

Acknowledgments

There are probably as many ways to write up an acknowledgments section as there are people I need to recognize. To make sure that I do not forget anyone, let me chronologically reflect on my development to this point (October 2, 2004). I'll start with a few people who influenced my decision to enter graduate school and go all the way up to present colleagues and friends.

First, I have to give props to my man Charlton Coles. Charlton was the first of my high school clique ("PSI-Inc") to finish his Ph.D., in psychology at the University of Florida, thereby setting the pace for the rest of us. I'd also like to thank my former engineering co-workers (especially Eric Babcock) for joining Charlton in encouraging me to pursue my sociological interests, even though this seemed crazy at the time.

There are a number of people who I hung out with in the early years at Indiana University who helped me realize that I was in the right place: my s558 methods group (Connie Rutledge, Keri Lubell, and Yolanda Zepeda), "Scubed" (Roxanna Harlow, Leslie Berg, Jeff Elder, Karen Lutfey, and Jeremy Freese), the "Race and Ethnic Studies Subaltern" (RESS) (Rox, Leslie, Jeff, Susan Oehler, and Jean Shin), Philip and Ann Holden-Moses, Roopali Mukherjee, Crystal Price, and Susan "Novie" Arias. Thank you for keeping me sane.

During my last two years at Indiana University I conducted and wrote up the autoethnography that provides the foundation of this book. From this period I would like to thank Dwight Brooks for keeping my cultural studies flights of fancy in check, Bill Corsaro for showing me how to fully harness the power of ethnography, Tom Gieryn for being my theoretical guru and all-around active sounding board, and Donna Eder for keeping the big picture in focus at all time. I could not have done the project without my assistants, Lori Canada, Rob Perez, Beeta Homaifar, Anna Lindzy, and Jennifer Richie. Thanks for an enjoyable and stimulating experience, gang! I must also mention Kevin Stewart for giving me a place to stay in the 1997–1998 academic year, and for letting me use his Miata.

There are three groups of people who have been influential ever since I entered higher education in 1986. First, I'd like to thank my family (especially Dad, Keith, and Evelyn) for all the support you've given. Second, to the professors who served as mentors and role models (Tom, Donna, Dwight, Jason Jimerson, Richard Corbin, and Brian "The Godfather" Powell), I will always try to keep it real. Third, my "Minnesota Connection" (Tamara Benjamin, Tom Zirps, and Kim Wapola) contains some of my oldest friends, who've known and supported me since my college days at Georgia Tech. Since arriving at the University of Minnesota in 1999 the Minnesota Connection has expanded to include Jehanne Beaton, Tamara, Terry Collins, Greg and Cathy Choy, Jeffrey Di Leo, Pat James, Amy Lee, Karen Miksch, Jeff Nygaard, Mark Pedelty, Connie, Kim, Marcia Williams, Beryl Wingate, Tom, and the newest member, my wife Valerie Minor. Thank you all for helping me to complete this book and launch exciting new projects.

Finally, I would like to thank all the students who have taken my classes over the years. You have provided me with a very rich experience, and inspire me to enter the classroom each day expecting wonderful possibilities. Thank you for helping me to speak the lower frequencies.

Chapter One

Entering the Pensieve

Toward the end of the class I asked the students if "the opportunity to get rid of the nig-
gas" was a possible justification for the trade. It is the first time I used that term this se-
mester. It slipped off the tongue pretty easily, especially as (at that point) I was pretty
frustrated at them being firmly entrenched in their Whiteness in all its erased glory.
Perhaps they were a bit scared to voice opinions, even after repeated comments from me
that it's ok to disagree with me, that it would not count against them. Moreso, though,
it is Whiteness as absence: don't see racial implications, would vote no 'cause it's "the
right thing to do."   —ETHNOGRAPHIC FIELD NOTE, 1997

The classroom is one of the most dynamic work settings precisely because we are given
such a short amount of time to do so much. To perform with excellence and grace teach-
ers must be totally present in the moment, totally concentrated and focused.
                                     —BELL HOOKS, *Teaching Community*

Should potentially explosive language and perspectives such as those
expressed in the ethnographic field note be used in introductory college
courses? What happens when teachers become (perhaps) *too* totally
present in the moment, in an effort to more fully engage students on
multiple levels, as I did in the field note regarding the film *Space Traders*,
in which the citizens of the United States vote to trade all African
Americans (like me) in exchange for new technologies from extraterrestrial aliens? What happens when we use ethnography (participant observation research) to both create and study contexts where teachers deploy theory to complicate and extend lived understandings of social
realities? In short, we theorize and empirically create the classroom as a
context in which both students and instructor(s) attempt to comprehend

and use language, power, and authority productively in democratic and humane forms in the physical classroom—and beyond. We create "Pensieves," classrooms in which the participants implode public and private ideas and experiences of who they were, are, and could be. In such a classroom teacher/researchers construct themselves as objects as well as subjects of study, helping individuals and groups negotiate the ever-expanding complexities of life in hyperdimensional societies. This book investigates these complexities as lived and learned in college classrooms as Pensieves.

If we are to make the classroom more democratic and, by extension, encourage students to be more critical and engaged citizens, we should experiment with new course forms and processes along these lines (Grossberg 1994; A. Kumar 1997; Lee 2000). We should attempt to use the cultural studies dicta of "the necessary detour through theory" and "engaging the concrete in order to change it" to more critically explore everyday life (Morley and Chen 1996; Turner 1996). The concept of "the Pensieve"—introduced in the fourth book in the popular *Harry Potter* children's series—may offer one possibility:

"At these times," said Dumbledore, indicating the stone basin, "I use the Pensieve. One simply siphons the excess thoughts from one's mind, pours them into the basin, and examines them at one's leisure. It becomes easier to spot patterns and links, you understand, when they are in this form." (Rowling 2000:597)

Rowling describes the Pensieve as a stone basin that stores human ideas and experiences. Harry Potter and others can then enter the basin to critically examine their ideas and experiences. I believe that the notion of the Pensieve can be used as a metaphor for a particular type of class experience,[1] one in which the instructor deconstructs the participants' (instructor and students) understandings in a way that makes invisible components visible. Specifically, instructors establish themselves as models for possible articulation of ideas and experiences in a particular time and place, in such a way that students can explore these ideas and experiences in other times and places. This revolves around what I call "the three EXs": teachers *expose* students to multiple narratives that involve the teachers' own lived experiences, *explode* those narratives into their constitutive parts based on structural locations (race, class, gender, sexual orientation, etc.), and *explicate* possible new narratives that explore implications of combinations of the constitutive parts (Jacobs 1998). In other words, teachers center ourselves (share articulations) in order to encourage students to displace us (create disarticulations) and center themselves (generate rearticulations) to explore their own understandings, identities, and practices. Teachers share "personal narratives to remind folks that we are all struggling to raise our consciousness and figure out the best action to take" (hooks 2003:107). Telling and listening to stories about social pasts, presents, and futures, "when juxtaposed with existential experiences, makes it possible to expose and interrogate cultural inscription and to reconsider and construct culture anew" (Garoian 1999:5).

When I show *Space Traders* to my classes, for example, there is usually a sharp divide and intense debate (though no fistfights . . . yet) between those who believe that the trade would never be accepted and those who stress that blacks should go ahead and pack their bags. I am, inevitably, called upon to settle the score: which interpretation is "correct"? The first step in creating a Pensieve is to deliberately disrupt easy closure: I argue for a probable outcome in a given (spatial as well as temporal) context, but stress that even then I can't put money in the bank. The goal here, of course, is to develop a stronger sense of the nature of power and discourse in America, that we must thoroughly deconstruct truth claims and the positions of authorities, even of college professors. Usually, further, the "trade won't happen" folks are disproportionately white, and the "done deal" people are of color (especially African Americans). As an African American instructor, I am placed in an intriguing position. Consider a juxtaposition of fragments from Paul Beatty's novel *The White Boy Shuffle* (1996):

I was the funny, cool black guy. In Santa Monica, like most predominantly white sanctuaries from urban blight, "cool black guy" is a versatile identifier used to distinguish the harmless black male from the Caucasian juvenile while maintaining politically correct semiotics. (p. 27)

Scoby is sitting on a stool listening to Sarah Vaughan. That's all he listens to now. . . . So I ask what's so special about Sarah. "Sarah's not one of those tragic niggers white folks like so much. Sarah's a nigger's nigger, she be black coffee. Not no mocha peppermint kissy-kissy butter rum do-you-have-any-heroin caffe latte." (p. 194)

I am frequently called upon by whites to be a "funny, cool, black guy" who will assure them that such a thing as voting to decide the fate of an historically oppressed people will never happen, and, perhaps, absolve them of any guilt that may be lingering about past realities. In Shelby Steele's (1990:10–11) terms, I am called upon to put on the mask of "bargainer": "I already believe that you are innocent (good, fairminded) and have faith that you will prove it." The students of color, on the other hand, want me to put on Steele's "challenger" mask: "if you [whites] are innocent, then prove it"; America is still a thoroughly racist place. Wearing the challenger mask also bolsters my position as a "nigger's nigger," who will toe the company (anti-integrationist) line. Rather than choosing between the two perspectives, in a Pensieve students and instructors explore a both/and perspective, analyzing how aspects of both constructions operate within an overarching hegemonic framework. As part of this process, I relate my own complexities within social forces such as race, demonstrating how context affects my thoughts and feelings: in some places I am a "bargainer" (e.g., as an untenured person discussing multiculturalism in faculty meetings), while in others I'm a "challenger" (e.g., as a citizen in anti-police brutality marches). In essence, I deliberately provide a model students can read to see how social representations and cultural products are used to create individual identities. I show my students how I combine elements of my experiences to support particular interpretations in an effort to encourage students to consider how they use their social locations (age, gender, race, ethnicity, class, sexual orientation, etc.) to make sense of their own practices and understandings. I am, in short, a "funny, cool, black guy" as well as a "nigger's nigger," with the strength of each particular flavor dependent on daily conditions.

Such a fluid construction and display of identity is facilitated by the "postmodern" condition of contemporary American society, where life is structured by "television-structured reality, the commodification of everyday life, the absence of meaning and the omnipresence of endless information, the relentless fascination with catastrophes, and the circulating advertisements for the death of the author, referent, and objective reality set within image upon image of the electronic connections among life, death, and sex" (Gordon 1997:13–14). In such a place it's very easy for students to become numb, to believe that their lives are not their own to control. Michel de Certeau (1997/1974:31), for instance, argues, "spectators are not the dupes of the media theater, but they refuse to say so." This should not be read reductively, that students always passively accept truth and knowledge claims disseminated by authority figures and formations. On the contrary, "in the postmodern, hegemony is won not simply through the transmission of ideas and the control of the population through centralization and homogenization; it operates also through the *abundance of choice* and the resulting fragmentation of the populace" (Sholle and Denski 1993:300, emphasis in original). Students engage in constant active selection of multiple alternatives, but they sometimes need help in making their choices more informed.

Students know the codes of the operation of difference in media and understand themselves through ubiquitous construction of the Other

(McLaughlin 1996), but they are less likely to admit that these under-standings are the result of struggle within an unevenly occupied terrain of struggle in which some groups have more power to construct favor-able representations of themselves and unfavorable accounts of others, and that these social constructions have very real material and cultural effects beyond the personal (Fiske 1994a, 1994b; Giroux 1996, 1994; Kellner 2003, 1995a, 1995b). One of the tasks of a Pensieve is to con-struct alternative representations as a means toward leveling social and cultural conditions; members can learn to organize new ways of think-ing into new ways of doing. This project involves constant discussion of how specific connections of elements of societal issues and personal beliefs serve particular interests and powers, and that these connec-tions are not "natural," that they are created through discourse and can be broken through discourse, and replaced with different understand-ings (Hall 1996; Hebdige 1996; Slack 1996). Participation in Pensieves helps students explicitly say that they are not dupes and explore ways to live as more empowered community members.

Theory into Practice

Consider the following set of quotations:

A media culture has emerged in which images, sounds, and spectacles help produce the fabric of everyday life, dominating leisure time, shaping political views and social behavior, and providing the materials out of which people forge their very identities. . . . Media stories and images provide the symbols, myths, and resources which help constitute a common culture for the majority of individuals in many parts of the world today. (Kellner, 1995a: 1)

For it is still the case that no one lives in the world in general. Everybody, even the exiled, the drifting, the diasporic, or the perpetually moving, lives in some confined and limited stretch of it—"the world around here." The sense of interconnectedness imposed on us by the mass media, by rapid travel, and by long-distance communication obscures this more than a little. . . . The banal-ities and distractions of the way we live now lead us, often enough, to lose sight of how much it matters just where we are and what it is to be there. (Geertz, 1996: 262)

Rather than empowering students to express their opinions, it seems more im-portant to give them information and skills that allow them to gather informa-tion from disparate sources, analyze it, and formulate informed evaluations, since critical thought involves understanding where "opinions" come from in the first place. (Stabile, 1997: 213)

Kellner's point calls attention to the pervasiveness of electronic media in American life. Increasingly, we generate understandings of who we were, are, and should be through appropriation and manipulation of electronically mass-mediated representations and ideas (see also Fiske 1994a; Miller 1998; Shaviro 2003). Geertz interjects that this process happens "somewhere," however, that it is not the same always and everywhere, but takes on locally distinct flavorings. Stabile outlines a main point we must consider if such local space is the college class-room: in postmodern conditions information about information some-times becomes more privileged than information itself (Harvey 1990); the job of teachers is to help students learn to juxtapose and make flex-ible connections of wildly disparate sources of ideas and experiences.

The members of Pensieves don't exist in vacuums, however. That is, their ideas and experiences are affected by their social histories and ma-terial conditions of life. In "The Eighteenth Brumaire of Louis Bona-parte," Karl Marx teaches us that people "make their own history, but they do not make it just as they please; they do not make it under circumstances chosen by themselves, but under circumstances directly found, given, and transmitted from the past" (Tucker 1978:595).[2] Simi-larly, Pensieves are constrained temporally, spatially, and materially. Participants attempt to create the space by juxtaposing many different ideas, conditions, and understandings, in the process debating not only acceptable fragments for inclusion, but questioning the rules of inclu-sion/exclusion themselves, under unequal discursive conditions. In Pensieves we are constantly sketching, erasing, and resketching visions of social processes and products, searching for optimal manifestations.

During the 1997–1998 academic year I constructed my undergradu-ate "media and society" classes at a large midwestern public university (Indiana University) as Pensieves. Along with undergraduate assist-ants, I conducted an ethnographic analysis of both fall and spring courses in an attempt to (1) understand how students use the media and its products to form understandings about themselves and Others, and (2) build on the purpose of a college classroom as a place of learn-ing, to investigate strategies for developing critical thinking and action, helping students actively use mediated understandings in social inter-action in the classroom as well as other spaces. Students learned to rec-ognize the contingent and constructed character of their representa-tions and understandings, considering how some understandings get stabilized, transposed, and even naturalized—all at the expense of other perspectives. The project included (a) teacher and undergradu-ate assistant observational data on classroom student–student and student-teacher interactions, (b) analysis of classroom assignments designed to encourage critical engagement with media and mediated information, and (c) analysis of meta-discursive data (comments on the course and classroom dynamics, such as in the course's electronic conferencing system).

Additionally (as I will detail extensively in chapter 2), I attempted to explore "autoethnographic" territory by investigating the implications of the insertion of the researcher into the very center of the study, as opposed to his or her more traditional detached perspective. Participation in postmodern media culture involves hyperreflexivity; a study of the classroom as a site of lived media culture demands that the instructor/researcher be as much an empirical object/subject as the students and media texts. Specifically, I am interested in how and to what extent students used me and my articulation of my experiences and understandings as a model for investigating their own feelings and knowledges, both inside and outside the classroom. I use this "teacher as text" strategy in an attempt to make an *intervention* in social worlds, refashioning webs of social relations to try to increase both personal and collective agency of the Pensieve's participants. Overall, six themes emerged over the course of the autoethnographic year and in subsequent years of continually evolving pedagogical practice.

1. *Students know media culture's individual products and processes, but need help in establishing systemic understandings.* Thomas McLaughlin (1996) argues that today's college students do the "theory" of making connections of media and mediated texts and their own experiences, but that this is often nonsystematic, and can (and should) be more rigorous; they are critical of media as pertaining to their individual lives only. When exposed to various texts such as newspaper editorials, World Wide Web sites, and TV commercials, students quickly pick out main themes and internal logics of the texts, but are less aware of how these texts are structured by and structure larger cultural systems of social life. I encourage students to resist, transform, and appropriate mediated understandings, instead of passively absorbing messages of who they should be and how they should act within social categorization (race, gender, class, sexual orientation, etc.). As each semester progresses, students became more adept at making systemic connections between their personal biographies and group structural locations.

2. *Critical media literacy is structured by social locations (age, gender, race, class, sexual orientation, etc.).* On the surface, this theme is a banality, as its basic operation is espoused in every study of the reception and

use of media. Henry Giroux (1993:368), for instance, argues that "literacy is a discursive practice in which difference becomes crucial for understanding not simply how to read, write, or develop aural skills, but also how to recognize that the identities of 'others' matter as part of a progressive set of politics and practices aimed at the reconstruction of democratic public life." This discursive practice is not only based on who the students "are" (men/women, white/black, straight/queer, etc), but on how they understand these personal identities in conjunction with the operation of Others, symbolically as well as in lived social interaction. I explore how and why some students operationalize a critical literacy surrounding first-time exposure to ideas and experiences, whereas others juxtapose and extend old ideas and practices in new ways. To be sure, there are many similarities in the two models, but the difference has an important implication: we must theorize and explore multiple strategies for understanding critical literacies, both as singularities and interactive units.

3. *Each class functions as a heuristic.* I not only want to teach students to learn and live media culture critically in my classroom, but to apply lessons learned to other spheres of life. Students learn that (1) all media are manufactured products, (2) all media are different, (3) media is big business, (4) media have values, and (5) audiences are different (Dover and Greene 1997:69; see also other articles in Hazen and Winokur 1997), and that these understandings can help them negotiate the processes of many spheres of life. Analysis of student media journals, course evaluations, and discussions with me (face-to-face and via e-mail) suggest that many students have begun to apply understandings created in my classroom to other situations, most often to their approach to other classes, but also in nonacademic settings as well.

4. *Elements of political economy, textual analysis, and ethnographic reception are all rolled into rigorous empirical study.* Lawrence Grossberg (1996) argues that Hall's (1980) encoding/decoding model of communication has spawned a hegemonic tripartite approach to the study of culture (including that of media): review of relevant institutions and practices governing production and distribution of particular texts, semiotic analysis of encoded meanings of those texts, and ethnographic studies of decodings and uses of the texts by individuals in their everyday lives. He claims that usually only one or two of the components are explored, and even if all three are explored such an

approach ends up "constantly rediscovering what it already knew" (p. 141) at the expense of engaging the newer and more important questions of social life under postmodern conditions. While I do not conduct a full-blown actualization of the tripartite approach, I do avoid the common mechanistic, reductionistic implementation of this method, and deploy the central elements of each to create a detailed analysis of the Pensieve in practice.

5. *The "teacher as text" concept is introduced and empirically investigated.* One may argue that the critical pedagogy project (see Gallop 1996; Giroux and McLaren 1994; Lankshear and McLaren 1993; Lee 2000; McLaren 1995; McLaughlin 1996) advocates that teachers get out of the center of teaching and learning. In such projects, the literacies, practices, and aspirations of students are the point of departure for helping student and teacher both construct a critical pedagogy of the everyday. My "teacher as text" strategy, on the other hand, uses the teacher(s)' worlds as the gateway. In part, this means exploring how the messenger affects an existing message (Moore 1997), but it also means that we examine how the message itself is dependent on the construction of the messenger. For instance, many students tell me that I am their first African American instructor. They are astonished when I use personal experiences with racism to help illustrate racism in the media; some accuse me of harboring "bias" and racism myself. I respond that there is not one racism, but many racisms, and that the choice of one definition over others reflects personal and group positions and interests. I relate how I resist a simple "Blacks can't be racist because we lack institutional power" definition for one that complicates "power," that considers intersections of race, gender, and class. I encourage students, in turn, to consider the implications— good and bad—of accepting one definition of racism while rejecting others. Establishing the teacher as a text, in sum, subverts traditional understandings of authority; authority as the embodiment of valued social characteristics (age, gender, race, ethnicity, etc.) is replaced by authority as the ability to create contexts that resonate on a lived level of consciousness. I explore how the deployment of the teacher as text affects the construction of the college classroom as Pensieve.

6. *"Autoethnography" is used to merge the analytical, the procedural, the imaginative, and the effervescent.* As previously noted, this book is concerned with the creation and documentation of the college classroom as Pensieve. In a way, the practices explored in the following chapters are classically experimental in that they put forth a hypothesis (one

can structure a classroom in such a way to encourage students to powerfully use media culture to increase agency) and "tests" it. "Autoethnography" constructs an ironic twist: not only is the hypothesis a test of a possible end, it is an open-ended means under constant construction. This book, then, describes continual play between the formation of symbolic desires and the discovery of material realities; it explores how the negotiation of meaning is both enabled and constrained. Autoethnography merges conceptual, theoretical, political, and methodological issues and procedures into a framework that not only tells us what was, but helps us imagine what can be.

Steven Shaviro argues: "We live in a world of images and sound. The electronic media are to us what 'nature' was to earlier times. That is to say, the electronic media are the inescapable background against which we live our lives and from which we derive our references and meanings" (2003:64). In such a world students must use electronic media and electronically mediated texts to learn and practice critical literacy, "the interpretation of the social present for the purpose of transforming the cultural life of certain groups, for questioning tacit assumptions and unarticulated presuppositions of current cultural and social formations and the subjectivities and capacities for agenthood that they foster" (McLaren and Lankshear 1993:413; see Lankshear and McLaren 1993 for other usages of the term). The identification and analysis of classroom interaction strategies and procedures surrounding students' engagement with media and mediated products increase the ability of the students to negotiate ever-expanding electronic media cultures. American society in general may benefit from increased knowledge of how electronic media cultures are understood and negotiated by student-citizens. This book builds on established research on media, pedagogy, postmodernity, and culture, and will suggest new directions for future investigation.

Chapter Outline

The process of narrating a personal experience that can be understood as part of a shared history or community memory is also empowering, not only for the speakers, but also for listeners. —KAMALA VISWESWARAN, *Fictions of Feminist Ethnography*

Following Visweswaran, my retelling of specific experiences is meant not only to detail how the students, my assistants, and I were or were not affected by classroom events, it encourages you—the readers—to create empowering perspectives. Most of the experiences I explore in this book come from the autoethnographic project at Indiana University (1997–1998) and its replication at the University of Minnesota (2000–2001), but I have been creating Pensieves since the first time I stepped into the classroom as a teacher (1995) and will do so until I exit in, oh, thirty years or so; this book contains illustrations of practice from the past as well as what I hope to do in the future.

In chapter 2, I will go into much greater conceptual and theoretical depth about Pensieves, specifically as applicable to the college classroom in public universities. In chapter 2 I will also discuss my notion of the teacher as text and my understanding of autoethnography. I will also flesh out the discussion of methodology employed for simultaneously teaching and researching social science/cultural studies courses.

Chapters 3, 4, 5, and 6 provide empirical illustration to the primarily abstract chapter 2. In each of these chapters I offer thick description (Geertz 1973) of "what happened" when I exposed students to a media text, exploded the text into its constitutive parts, and explicated resulting understandings into possible larger frameworks of interpretation. I detail both successes and failures in this effort, and utilize data generated by use of other texts to complete the analysis of the central main text. Chapters 3, 4, 5, and 6 are more than "data" chapters, however, as each one significantly extends and expands understanding of theoretical and methodological arguments begun in chapter 2. As heuristics, these chapters are designed to be open for continual negotiation and renegotiation, and generate different perspectives when read in different "moments," spatially and temporally bound contexts of interpretation.

Each chapter is a moment that details particular intersections of text (media products) and context (classroom and campus communities). The central media texts themselves, additionally, are chosen to analyze three different forms of "text" employed in the study. Although all texts are fragments of larger historical and social conditions (Eco 1994), chapter 3 explores the use of texts that are not meant to stand alone; the texts of this chapter are pieces extracted from coherent and explicitly bounded products. The chapter centers around my use of a seven-minute slice of the two-hour film *I Like It Like That* to measure student entry into "the matrix of domination," the space where we examine intersections of both social privilege and cultural domination. *I Like It Like That* is about the lives of a Puerto Rican family in New York City; I exposed the seven-minute clip (about webs of race, gender, and class) to students multiple times over a semester and analyzed the change (or

lack thereof) of their critical responses. I also analyze in-class exploration of print advertisements and music (videos and tracks from CDs).

Chapter 4, on the other hand, is concerned with the reception of entire putatively stand-alone products. The central text of this chapter is
the forty-minute film *Space Traders* and the short story from which the
film is adapted. In both texts the citizens of the United States vote to
trade all African Americans to extraterrestrial aliens in exchange for
new technologies. I investigate student reactions to my efforts to make
such texts "strange," pointing out unremarked aspects and leading
them in investigations of the intertextuality of the texts, that to fully
comprehend individual products we depend on knowledge of other
texts and experiences, and that we should explicitly explore the implications of particular articulations of these knowledges and perspectives. I explore reception of an episode of the television show *The X-
Files* to complement the analysis of *Space Traders*.

Chapter 5 explores the moment in which the context is the text. That
is, from time to time I would ask students to explicitly and reflexively
ponder how being in a sociology class affected readings of a text that we
were collectively experiencing. I focus on "storytelling days," in which I
read short stories to the class and lead discussion about the story and the
process of the oral storytelling itself, connecting it to overarching
systems of privilege and domination. Secondarily, I analyze meta-
discursive data concerning classes held outside the normal classroom, in
which small groups of students met with me at a campus restaurant for
an hour at a time, in lieu of attending a regular class session.

Chapter 6 looks at students' and assistants' understandings of the
Pensieve upon completion of a course with me. In the year after taking a
"media and society" course, twelve former Indiana University students
met with me and one assistant in a weekly focus group on *The X-Files*:
they watched each episode on their own and then we met in groups at a
local restaurant to discuss the episode and any social issues it raised.
The goal, however, was not so much to generate a close textual analysis
of each episode; it was to use elements from the show and the previous
year's "media and society" course to stimulate reflection on wider social
contexts. I discuss how a small weekly salon about a TV show like *The X-
Files* provides the participants with the space, time, and raw materials to
ask and answer tough questions about themselves and society. The
chapter also presents the assistants' analyses of their experiences with
the focus group and/or the 1997–1998 autoethnography.

In chapters 3–6 I include two stand-alone sections in which I focus
on a single student. In each of these chapters I provide a sketch of one

student (using data from in-class observations, course assignments, and the student's direct communication with me) who embraced the forwarded media literacy strategies, and a sketch of one student who resisted these dynamics. I do this not only to offer further analysis of both successes and failures of the project, but also to add a personal, individualistic complement to the composites of students I predominantly use in the book.

Finally, chapter 7 concludes the book by examining experimental techniques deployed at the University of Minnesota: (1) a fall 2000 failure concerning strange texts, (2) a spring 2001 use of a sophomore undergraduate teaching assistant, and (3) a spring 2002 twist on storytelling. The book wraps up with an unusual definition of "evocation." In the end, the Pensieve creates a beginning that sends us on a never-ending journey.

Seeing Invisibilities, Speaking Lower Frequencies

I am an invisible man. . . . I am invisible, understand, simply because people refuse to see me. . . . When they approach me they see only my surroundings, themselves, or figments of their imagination—indeed, everything and anything except me.
—RALPH ELLISON, *Invisible Man*

[T]here's a possibility that even an invisible man has a socially responsible role to play. . . . Being invisible and without substance, a disembodied voice, as it were, what else could I do? What else but to try to tell what was really happening when your eyes were looking through? And it is this which frightens me: Who knows but that, on the lower frequencies, I speak for you? —RALPH ELLISON, *Invisible Man*

Created under the very nose of the overseers, the utopian desires which fuel the contemporary politics of transfiguration must be invoked by other, more deliberately opaque means. This politics exists on a lower frequency where it is played, danced, and acted, as well as sung and sung about, because words, even words stretched by melisma and supplemented or mutated by the screams which still index the conspicuous power of the slave sublime, will never be enough to communicate its unsayable claims to the truth.
—PAUL GILROY, *The Black Atlantic*

Social theorists of many ages have claimed that we frequently manipulate past understandings with visions of desired future scenarios to create present realities; theorists of postmodernity emphasize the electronic mediation (by TV, film, music, the Internet, etc.) of these articulations, and investigate their existence within a vast consumer culture

(Kellner 2003, 1995a). A postmodern space, hence, is a discursive arena in which we use electronically produced and/or consumed mass market images, sounds, and spectacles to create fleeting, fragmented understandings of ourselves and our values, purposes, and truths. Moreover—as the epigraphs of this section suggest—those living in capitalist postmodern societies like America "choose" to not fully explore the complexities of power in their existence. Such societies are saturated with power as power/knowledge (Foucault 1980:142): "power is co-extensive with the social body . . . relations of power are interwoven with other kinds of relations . . . these relations don't take the sole form of prohibition and punishment, but are of multiple forms . . . dispersed, heteromorphous, localised procedures of power are adapted, re-inforced and transformed by these global strategies . . . power relations do indeed 'serve' . . . because they are capable of being utilized in strategies . . . [and] there are no relations of power without resistances." In an America where even the most countercultural messages are eventually reappropriated by big business (Frank 1997), students must learn how to strategically use power/knowledge in a never-ending project to articulate new ideas and possibilities.

In Pensieves the participants learn to hear and speak on lower frequencies than they usually tune: they learn to say that they are not cultural dupes and reveal hard-to-discern traces of social structures, exploring how individuals and groups shape and are shaped by multiple social events and practices. Participants study capitalism "to expose its mechanisms of inequality, to motivate people to change them, and to reveal sites and methods by which change might be promoted" (Fiske 1994b:198). Both students and teachers construct tools to comprehend chaotic social experiences and knowledges. They create heuristics.

Members of Pensieves use the heuristics to etch all sorts of ideas about social worlds onto a communal screen. A Pensieve is a palimpsest in which uncovering earlier social tracings can be quite important, guiding not only present but future markings. We may not ever know exactly what the palimpsest's etchings are supposed to represent, but must make attempts to delineate common—if temporary—possibilities.[3] Many people attempt to ignore earlier inscriptions, but if we learn to recognize them and incorporate them into future negotiations we can empower our surroundings and ourselves. We must learn to think sociologically: "the increasingly sophisticated understandings of representation and of how the social world is textually or discursively constructed still require an engagement with the social structuring practices that have long been the province of sociological inquiry" (Gordon 1997:11; see also Clough 1992). Such inquiries draw attention to both visible and invisible—and spoken and silent—forces and ideas that hegemonically shape our national and local cultures and realities.

In this book I provide many different fragments of material and discursive realities that unfolded in my classes, and juxtapose them (with each other as well as with outside fragments, such as quotes from scholarly papers and books) in ways that explore sociological significances of postmodern conditions of existence. I encourage readers to combine the stories told within with their own stories, not only to evaluate the potency and efficacy of the social processes detailed here, but of analogous issues and ideas, in both similar and different contexts than the college classroom of large public universities. Compare and contrast sketches to grasp and appreciate other ways of knowing and seeing. Use this project to rethink "objectivity":

To be objective is not just to tolerate another's epistemic culture, but to engage in cross-the-border conversations, selectively borrowing what works for you, perhaps seeking to persuade the other of the utility of your knowledge for their projects (success at this can not be guaranteed), never imposing your epistemic culture by force of gun or pretensions of privilege (i.e., rationality, truth, moral purity, standpoint), and using the encounter to examine ceaselessly the foundations and implications of one's own knowledge-making practices. (Gieryn 1994:325)

If the United States continues to become a multicultural nation that is bombarded with a rich set of mediated representations of who we were, are, and should be, then we need such understandings of objectivity to enable us to lead truly democratic lives. I attempt to create spaces in which the participants grapple with the myriad intricacies (with both negative and positive spins) that arise in this project. I sketch some of them now, in an effort to help us all learn to continually re-sketch them in powerfully productive ways.

Chapter Two

Autoethnography of Teachers, Texts, and Space

What distinguishes cultural studies, I would argue, is its radical contextualism. In fact, cultural studies, in its theoretical practice, might be described as a theory of contexts, or, in its practice, as the practice of making contexts.
— LAWRENCE GROSSBERG, "Bringing it All Back Home"

One thing really bothered me in the beginning of the course, and I even stopped coming for a while. Walt always brought whatever topic we were on into a racial/cultural debate. He always talked about cultural studies and not enough sociology or, as titled, "MEDIA in society." — STUDENT RESPONSE, 1997 course evaluation

When we think of a large college classroom for an introductory course, we often imagine a static place, a space where students imbibe nuggets of knowledge dished out by the sage on the stage, to be regurgitated a few weeks later for dissection by graduate student assistants. In a classroom as Pensieve, however, we create a new context in which students and instructor(s) explore a different understanding of teaching and learning. We put critical pedagogical principles into practice: "critical pedagogy is concerned with revealing, interrogating, and challenging those legitimated social forms and opening the space for additional voices" (Alexander 1999:307). Students explicitly say that they are not passive dupes, and attempt to comprehend and use culture and power reflexively in the physical classroom, and beyond. The classroom becomes a space of "radical possibility" (hooks 2003, 1994a), in which the members "invent and explore counterdiscourses to formulate oppositional interpretations of their identities, interests, and needs" (Fraser

1992:123). In a classroom as Pensieve the participants speak the lower frequencies.

As noted in the epigraph, there is a lot of resistance to this effort, as (among other things) students resist the blurring of disciplinary boundaries and the placement of everyday experiences into larger theoretical and social contexts. Through years of socialization about the educational process, they have come to expect not only specific forms of course content, but specific ways in which that content is presented. If we are to make the classroom a place where students can critically interrogate such socialization, we have to deploy experimental course processes such as the Pensieve, and record the results using methods like ethnography to capture a rich set of hopes and fears, exhilarations and frustrations, successes and failures.

The challenges surrounding this project are not only present in the creation of Pensieves, they affect efforts to convey the results of such experimentation, given that the conditions of late modernity/postmodernity have altered both the investigation and reporting of group communication and culture: we can no longer be sure (if we ever were) that our representations correspond to an external, objective "reality" (Clifford and Marcus 1986, Clough 1992, Denzin 1997). Norman Denzin (1997:247) argues that

Ethnographies will be empirical in the classical sense of the word based on the articulated experiences of people in concrete places. Ethnographies will not attempt to capture the totality of a group's way of life. The focus will be interpreted slices, glimpses, and specimens of interaction that display how cultural practices, connected to structural formations and narrative texts, are experienced at a particular time and place by interacting individuals.

In this chapter I will explain why and how this project works when constructing and analyzing college classrooms as Pensieves, centering on the effects of postmodern conditions on students' understandings and use of electronic media culture. I provide a heuristic, offering my account as a guide for others to use in their investigations of other postmodern spaces, of the classroom as well as other contexts: "Readers are put in the position of experiencing an experience that can reveal to them not only how it was for us but how it could be or once was for them. They are made aware of similarities and differences between their worlds and ours. It becomes possible for them to see the other in themselves or themselves in the other among other possibilities" (Ellis and Bochner 1994:98; see also Ronai 1994).

Further, I agree with Laurel Richardson (1993:706), who wonders "How valid can the knowledge of a floating head be?" She is referring to scholarly accounts that efface the researcher's emotions, lived values, and dreams, work that relies almost exclusively on reason and rationality. Knowledge and use of media involves more than the head, therefore I use the sociobiographical statuses and experiences of my co-ethnographers and myself to help capture how complicated, diverse, and intense perspectives and emotions that are generated in some classrooms may come together. This is one of the components of doing "autoethnography," which is the overarching method employed in researching my classes. I follow Clough (1992) in the attempt to use (auto)ethnography as social critique, especially given debate about the uses and roles of higher education under postmodern conditions (Apple 2000; Aronowitz 2000; Dellucchi and Smith 1997a, 1997b; Dumont 1995; Eisenberg 1997; Kolodny 1998; Kumar 1997; Nelson 1997a, 1997b; Shepperd 1997; Sweet 1998a, 1998b). I detail how my project of the "teacher as text" (Jacobs 1998) is a specific autoethnographic technique for critiquing as well as creating the classroom as Pensieve.

Finally, most of the empirical examples used in the book were generated in a 1997–1998 study of classes I taught at Indiana University, so I will explain specific methods used in that study. This includes (a) observational data collected by myself and five undergraduate assistants (Lori Canada, Beeta Homaifar, Anna Lindzy, Rob Perez, Jennifer Richie) on classroom student–student and student–teacher interactions, (b) analysis of classroom assignments designed to encourage critical engagement with electronic media and mediated information, and (c) analysis of meta-discursive data (comments on the course and classroom dynamics, such as in the course's electronic conferencing system(s)). Collectively, these three types of data yield a richly nuanced rendition of the Pensieve we created and inhabited in 1997–1998 at Indiana University, helped me fashion additional Pensieves at the University of Minnesota, and will provide grounding for future Pensieves yet to be born.

Postmodern Space

Post-modernity is modernity without the hopes and dreams which made modernity bearable. —DICK HEBDIGE, "Postmodernism and 'the Other Side'"

[W]e believe that at least certain strains of postmodern thinking are a key resource for rethinking a democratic social theory and politics.
—LINDA NICHOLSON AND STEVEN SEIDMAN, *Social Postmodernism*

In chapter 1 I said that "a postmodern space [such as a Pensieve] is a discursive arena in which we use electronically produced and/or

consumed mass market images, sounds, and spectacles to create fleeting, fragmented understandings of ourselves and our values, purposes,
and truths." The underlying connotation of "postmodernity" in this
sentence is neutral; one does not receive a sign to suggest whether this
is a positive or negative development. Many theorists of postmodernity
would say that this is the whole point, that "postmodernism" means
that signs and signifiers float free without any connections, and, more
to the point, it doesn't make sense to assign value to this condition—
this is just the way things are (Baudrillard 1994, 1988, 1983). Many others, however, while accepting the fluidity of signs and signifiers (this is
a characteristic that appears in most descriptions of postmodern conditions) believe that value should be attached to this development,
though it will be partial and pragmatic (reflecting contested grounded
interests instead of transcendental objectivity), and subject to debate
and action. It may emphasize negatives, as articulated earlier by Hebdige, or push us to consider positive manifestations, as Nicholson and
Seidman argue in the introduction to a volume that defends postmodern perspectives anchored in the cultures and politics of the new social
movements. Or, on a third hand, valuation may be attached to an am-
biguous position combining positives and negatives, such as tensions
between the modern and postmodern [such as Kellner 1995a and Harvey 1990), two versions of postmodernism (such as Rosenau's (1993) af-
firmative and skeptic camps, or Foster's (1983) resistance and reactionary formations] or even one modernism and two postmodernisms
[Lemert's (1997) radical modernism, radical postmodernism, and strategic postmodernism]. Indeed, combinations of perspectives and discussion of tensions are endless. Perhaps trying to describe postmodernism is a postmodern exercise in and of itself!

However it is used, and regardless of positive, negative, or neutral
spins, theories of postmodernism are all concerned with explaining a
possible fundamental change in Western society in which privileged
Westerners can no longer be sure—referentially *and* pragmatically—
that what we know is what we know:

The term *postmodernism* straddles several definitional boundaries. It refers at
once to a sensibility, a political perspective, a state of mind, and a mode of social analysis. Taking these as an amalgam, we may speak of the postmodern
age: an era wherein democratic imperatives have become subverted, ordinary
values simulated, and emancipatory symbols and their affective power com-
modified. It is an age in which the modernist quest for certainty and meaning
and the liberal humanist notion of the individual as a unified and coherent essence and agency are being forcefully challenged. (McLaren and Lankshear
1993:383; emphasis in original)

I wish to take such an understanding on postmodern thought as positive as my starting point for theoretically grounding the Pensieve. Why? First, following the essays in Nicholson and Seidman (1995), I believe that a focus on microlevel concerns of the everyday can be combined with institutional and cultural analyses to make interventions in an age in which time and space are "compressed," in which "the time horizons of both private and public decision-making have shrunk, while satellite communication and declining transport costs have made it increasingly possible to spread those decisions immediately over an ever wider and variegated space" (Harvey 1990:147).

Second, feminist versions of postmodernism remind us that hierarchies and oppressions still exist, even if increasingly mobile, partial, situated, and contested (Haraway 1990, 1991; Nicholson 1990). The knowledge produced in the Academy is often used to legitimate oppressive institutional practices and discourses, such as those of the military and prisons (Lubiano 1996). The work of academics, then, "has something to do with influencing how priorities are set by [institutions such as the state and multinational corporations] and with articulating how the U.S. national subject understands the nation's place in the world and its history" (Lubiano 1996:70).

Academics who are members of marginalized groups, especially, often feel compelled to explore ways of using our locations in the Academy to disrupt "the state's use of the intellectual and cultural productions of and about marginalized groups . . . [and explore] institutionally transformative possibilities for middle-class people of color affiliated with universities who, as I've suggested, are also themselves bound up with this state-sponsored knowledge" (Lubiano 1996:71; see also West 1990). Like all academics, scholars of color are caught up in webs of power/knowledge (Foucault 1980, 1978) that especially discipline historically marginalized groups; it is our task to work within and between discursive communities to develop resistances to further marginalization. Lubiano (1996:75) concludes that the university is like a fountain, where "the water is being poisoned right here at the epistemological well. It is important to make a stand right here at that well."

A strong component of that stand is the project of rethinking Jurgen Habermas's notion of the "public sphere" (Habermas 1989/1962). There is much scholarship on the natures, histories, and social implications of the theory and practice of this construct, the body of "private persons" assembled to debate matters of "public interest" in efforts to shape the "public good" (e.g., Calhoun 1992, Habermas 1989/1962, Kumar 1997, Robbins 1993, Weintraub and Kumar 1997). Among other things, debate revolves around the key assumptions of a Habermasian public sphere of bourgeois society: (1) participants attempt to bracket status differentials and interact as if they were social equals, (2) fragmentation into multiple public spheres is viewed as a move toward less democracy, (3) the appearance of private interests and issues is undesirable, and (4) there is a sharp division between civil society and the state (Fraser 1992:117–118).

Critiques of these tenets appear in many academic camps. First, for example, theorists of race, gender, and class argue that it is not possible to truly bracket social status designations and, thus, be able to act as neutral, objective, and disembodied agents (Anderson and Collins 1998; hooks 1994b, 1990); even in cyberspace discourse bears the trace of social location and experience, despite attempts to hide them (Miller 1995). Second, multiculturalists argue that a focus on a single public deflects scrutiny of the interactions of margins and centers, an awareness that centers shift and are won and lost through the struggles of formations of individuals, that "a center has no meaning apart from its dialogue with cast out and marginalized elements of a culture. . . . [M]ulticulturalism has demonstrated that there are always more stories than the dominant culture chooses to tell" (Nelson 1997a:127; see also Gordon and Newfield 1996). Third, feminist theory and practice have a long and powerful history of demonstrating that the private is intricately bound up in the public (Bartky 1990; Collins 1991; Faludi 1991; hooks 1990). Fourth, demonstrating critical links between civil society and the state was a central project of the civil rights movements and is continued in the work of the new social movements (Nicholson and Seidman 1995; Omi and Winant 1994).

In sum, academics from many walks of life are encouraged to theorize and operationalize multiple public spheres, as "in stratified societies, arrangements that accommodate contestation among a plurality of competing publics better promote the ideal of participatory parity than does a single, comprehensive, overarching public" (Fraser 1992:122). Fraser offers the notion of "subaltern counterpublic" as essential to the creation of strong multicultural identities and practices:

Historically, therefore, members of subordinated social groups—women, workers, peoples of color, and gays and lesbians—have repeatedly found it advantageous to constitute alternative publics. I have called these "subaltern counterpublics" in order to signal that they are parallel discursive arenas where members of subordinated social groups invent and circulate counterdiscourses. Subaltern counterpublics permit them to formulate oppositional interpretations of their identities, interests, and needs. (Fraser 1995:291)

Is this notion, however, useful for the classroom as Pensieve, especially when many students would not define themselves as subaltern?
Can it be used effectively in "border crossings" (Giroux 1992; see also
Anzaldua 1987) between academic and everyday worlds, and across
and among disparate cultures to encourage more democratic and humane understandings and interaction? Or, on the other hand, will it
contribute to neoconservative policies of stratification and inequality,
that is, a "conservative multiculturalism" of a surface understanding
of "valuing diversity" only in that it promotes capital accumulation
and stimulates further consumption (McLaren 1995)? In other words,
how can we facilitate the implementation of the classroom as a subaltern counterpublic that encourages teachers and students to explore
their differences in productive rather than destructive ways? How can
we create McLaren's (1995:126) "resistance multiculturalism," which
"doesn't see diversity itself as a goal but rather argues that diversity
must be affirmed within a politics of cultural criticism and a commitment to social justice"?

I offer two guidelines. First, members of Pensieves explore a "radical
democratic" approach to citizenship in late capitalist society: articulations about "the common good" are viewed as "'a vanishing point,'
something to which we must constantly refer when we are acting as
citizens, but can never be reached" (Mouffe 1995:326). A critical component of this is learning and living in and with the multiple interlaced relations of power introduced by our existence in expanding media (Kellner 2003, 1995a, 1995b) and consumer (Jameson 1983; Lury 1996)
cultures. We make our social worlds problematic, creating "problems
[that] would be significant to the extent that they raised questions for
individuals and groups in our society in ways that would not simply
underwrite a purely presentist orientation or a projective inclination to
rewrite the past in order to find mouthpieces or vehicles for currently
affirmed values" (LaCapra 1997:62). In Pensieves we teach our students—and remind ourselves—that particular articulations of perspectives and experiences have implications that go beyond our immediate
interests, and that the "common good" is always under negotiation and
affects different groups in divergent ways.

Second, we must enter the "matrix of domination" (Collins 1991).
While it is necessary for oppressed peoples to form oppositional
spaces, these efforts can lead to serious problems in both inter and
intragroup interaction. Internally, subaltern counterpublics can generate essentialist discourse, policing boundaries in destructive battles
with and/or to the exclusion of those who aren't "black enough," or

"queer enough," or "real leftists," and so on. Externally, such police action often leads to narrow identification with one axis of oppression, and squabbles over "whose oppression is greatest," and/or what combination of oppressions is more destructive (Berman 1994; Feagan et al. 1996; Gardner 1995; Wallace 1990; Warner 1993 [part II]). This is "identity politics" at its worst, and needs to be overcome (Haraway 1991; Nicholson and Seidman 1995). Collins offers us this invaluable lesson: no one is purely an "oppressor" or purely "privileged." We never reach a state in which we are not empowered vis-à-vis some Other group; we always exist in a cauldron in which sometimes we are oppressed and sometimes we are oppressors. We (like any and everyone else) must maintain eternal vigilance.

For instance, it is safer for us to focus on race as an essence, *or* as an illusion, but it is more productive—though much harder—to view it as a both/and dynamic (Omi and Winant 1994). Both the axes on which we are socially advantaged and ones on which we are socially disadvantaged may vary by context (temporally and spatially). We must investigate the multivalenced and contested operation of both privileged and subjugated identities and resulting experiences. We must strive to "illuminat[e] the various ways in which representations are constructed as a means of comprehending the past through the present in order to legitimate and secure a particular view of the future" (Giroux 1994:87).

The Pensieve, then, includes a specific purpose of contesting dominant social issues and ideals and empowering subordinated groups. Participants interrogate "hegemony," the process by which elite groups maintain ruling positions through securing the consent of the ruled (Gramsci 1971). In my "media and society" classes I devote special attention to the mediated operation of hegemony: "The contemporary popular media fragment, create dissensus, threaten, and erase the practical base of knowledge that marginal or powerless groups need in order to take hold of their everyday lives and work toward changing their historical conditions" (Sholle and Denski 1993:308). Each class explores the operation of difference in media, how we understand ourselves through ubiquitous construction of the Other, that these understandings are the result of struggle within an unevenly occupied terrain of struggle in which some groups have more power to construct favorable representations of themselves and unfavorable accounts of others, and that these social constructions have very real material and cultural effects (Bobo 1995; hooks 1994b; Gillespie 1995; Giroux 1994, 1996; Kellner 2003, 1995a, 1995b).

Sholle and Denski (1993:316) argue that the classroom is an important site "of struggle over the creation, recreation, and maintenance of our individual understanding of the values and relations which arise from our collective understanding of the past, present, and future," and that media texts can be used to help students both recognize the operation of hegemony and make counterhegemonic interventions. In Pensieves teachers and students alike learn the framework of this process and engage in such negotiation, with an eye toward applying lessons to other publics:

> [W]e grasp these processes not because we want to expose them or to understand them in the abstract but because we want to *use* them *effectively* to contest that authority and leadership by offering arguments and alternatives that are not only 'correct' ('right on') but convincing and convincingly presented, arguments that capture the popular imagination, that engage directly with the issues, problems, anxieties, dreams and hopes of real (actually existing) men and women: arguments, in other words, that take the popular (and hence the populace) seriously *on its own terms*. (Hebdige 1996:195, emphasis in original)

As a Pensieve each of my classes learns to deal with a postmodern condition in which "truth is highly elusive, [and] exits on multiple levels" (Kellner 2003:146); they explore the construction of alternative representations as a means of changing social and cultural realities.

Autoethnography

Bad Subjects autobiography is characterized by its focus on how personal experience is always embedded in social forces ranging from the economic to the domestic. We invite the reader to enter the life of another person, while simultaneously reflecting on the public landscape that inevitably shapes individual experience. The point is less to tell a personal story, than it is to explore how no story can ever be truly personal—common political ideas play a part in even our most private moments.
> —BAD SUBJECTS PRODUCTION TEAM, *Bad Subjects*

In order to fully implement Pensieves we need a method of recording what happens within, and "autoethnography" can meet that need. While discussions of "autoethnography" and "critical autobiography" are legion in specialized qualitative literature (such as Alexander 1999; Bochner and Ellis 2001; Ellis and Bochner 1996; Spry 2001), I believe that a fragment from a collection of essays from a 'zine devoted to revitalizing the Left best illustrates my vision of a method of simultaneously creating and studying a postmodern research context. I will examine each of the three sentences of the epigraph in turn, and conclude by adding a fourth point that completes a discussion of an autoethnography (as opposed to their "autobiography").

The first sentence calls attention to a point shared in all visions of autoethnography/autobiography: the author(s)' own personal experiences are foregrounded and investigated. Whereas, traditionally, "ethnographic observers and writers have looked across social and cultural differences, across boundaries, into the worlds of others as a means of laying claim to their own" (Neumann 1996:180), autoethnographic inquiry in which the author is subject *and* object (in interaction with other people and things) provides insights into the increasingly postmodern condition of fluidity and fragmentation, "when we acknowledge how much 'out there' looks a lot like 'in here'" (Neumann 1996:182), and where "subjectivity is based on liminal, contingent, and ephemeral practices through which culture, identity, and agency are continually critiqued and renegotiated" (Garoian 1999:10). Following Alexander (1999:310), "I approach ethnographic, autobiographic, and autoethnographic research as a way of reading between the lines of my own lived experience and the experiences of cultural familiars—to come to a critical understanding of self and other and those places where we intersect and overlap." We sometimes must read our own practices and worlds very closely to not only understand them, but larger social circles as well.

The investigations of the author(s)' own experiences are not done as narcissistic flights of fancy, wherein "a sort of 'vanity ethnography' results, in which only the private muses and demons of the fieldworker are of concern" (Van Maanen 1988:93). Exploration is carried out to create heuristics, as noted in the second sentence of the epigraph. By examining how particular structures, perspectives, and experiences created a social world in one time and place, readers are offered tools to critically examine and/or construct other social contexts. This is especially important if we have indeed entered postmodern conditions of flexible accumulation (Harvey 1990) and hyperreality (Baudrillard 1994), in which we are encouraged to think that we have considerable abilities to personalize and tailor our social worlds within global logics of consumption (Jameson 1983). Autoethnographic investigations help us challenge those claims; we negotiate dystopian as well as utopian manifestations of postmodern states.

The third sentence reminds us of the importance of foregrounding power [as Foucault's (1980, 1978) power/knowledge] in our analysis, specifically theorizing and empirically investigating the operation of the increasingly blurred boundaries of public and private. Autoethnographies make interventions into the operation of power in that they resist the effacement of public and private, and encourage those involved to make alternative articulations. Regarding media culture, for in-stance, "the media function by fragmenting the subject in order to pro-duce a 'knowing, cynical, self-constituting' viewer who nevertheless goes on consuming works by actually eliminating self-reflection" (Sholle and Denski 1993:315). Autoethnography can demonstrate why and how this process happens, how postmodern power moves away from repression and constraint, "it incites, it induces, it seduces" (Michel Foucault, cited in Shaviro 2003:6). I can help students say that they are not dupes by showing them why and how I say this: "Good autoethnography is not simply a confessional tale of self-renewal; it is a provocative weave of story and theory" (Spry 2001:713).

Combining these three points [autoethnography (1) situates author as subject and object, (2) establishes heuristics, and (3) calls attention to and intervenes in circuits of power] with the Pensieve's task of explor-ing interwoven intersections of societal categorization, we come up with a project that looks like Anne Balsamo's (1997:161) "feminist cul-tural studies": "The project of feminist cultural studies more broadly is to write the stories and tell the tales that will connect seemingly isolated moments of discourse—histories and effects—into a narrative that helps us make sense of transformation as they emerge."

Here we must add a fourth point to distinguish a critical autobiogra-phy from an autoethnography. One of the strengths of ethnography (in whatever form) is its careful and rigorous documentation of "what happened" as the researchers observe the field (Corsaro 1985; Van Maanen 1986). Whereas "autobiography" may be little more than recol-lection on random past events, "autoethnography" is a study by de-sign. Specifically, autoethnographers realize that their actions help shape social worlds, and design frameworks to capture and chart spe-cific ways in which the *collective* interaction of actors unfolded. This last point is not trivial: autoethnographies don't just capture isolated expe-riences and thoughts of the autoethnographers, but seek to explore and explain how those dynamics were created and what possible future ef-fects may accrue. Given that "people do not possess power but produce it and are produced by it in their relational constitution through dis-course" (McLaren and Lankshear 1993:382; see also Foucault 1980) it is imperative that autoethnographers chart and interrogate their own negotiation of power that they create and that creates them and their worlds. They must be reflexive throughout: "Reflexivity is not some-thing to be 'done' in an appendix or an introduction. To invite the reader to monitor one's reflexivity post *post hoc*, while suspending the display of it in the course of analytic practice, is merely another man-agement strategy masquerading as a solution" (Watson 1987:38 [note

10]). Note that "reflexive" is the word of choice here, not "reflective." Being reflective connotes contemplation after the fact; being reflexive means that "we need continually to interrogate and find strange the process of representation as we engage it" (Woolgar 1988:29). Reflexivity "checks the politics of cultural work and prevents ideological domination" (Garoian1999:9). Autoethnographers are not only conscious of themselves as Other, they are conscious of being self-conscious as Other (Babcock 1980; see also Marcus 1994).

My vision of autoethnography, then, "is an attempt to interpret the public and private dimensions of cultural experience and seek a critical distance and perspective on each" (Neumann 1996:192). When authors are objects and well as subjects, explicitly try to create heuristics, explore and critique operation of circuits of power, and frame all this within a reflexive and rigorous design, we gain increased understanding and critical flexibility in postmodern conditions of life.

The Teacher as Text

With and through articulation, we engage the concrete in order to change it. . . . Articulation, then, is not just a thing (not just a connection), but a process of creating connections, much in the same way that hegemony is not domination but the process of creating and maintaining consensus of co-ordinating interests.

—JENNIFER SLACK,
"The Theory and Method of Articulation in Cultural Studies"

Autoethnographies of educational spaces encourage critical thinking, in which "being critical means something more than simply fault-finding. It involves understanding the sets of historically contingent circumstances and contradictory power relationships that create the conditions in which we live" (Apple 2000:5). I developed a specific technique to facilitate such thinking in the college classroom as Pensieve: "the teacher as text" (Jacobs 1998). It is centered on the concept of "articulation" as elaborated in this section's epigraph (see also Morley and Chen 1996). Articulation helps us understand the two-way interaction of personal biography and the operation of social structure (both temporally and spatially) under postmodern conditions of increasing fragmentation, uncertainty, and mass-mediation. Quite simply, articulation tells us that (1) specific connections of elements of societal issues and personal troubles serve particular interests and powers, and (2) these connections are not "natural"—they are created through discourse and can be broken through discourse, and replaced with different understandings (Hall 1996).[1] In Pensieves teachers use their articulations of personal experiences and theoretical frameworks to help students make sense of their own perceptions and practices, and work toward creating more powerful understandings and actualization of agency.

Let me proceed by describing an incident from the summer of 1996, when I taught a sociology "race and ethnic relations" class. The incident details an e-mail from a female friend from the days before I entered academia, and my reactions to it. "I've decided that you are so out of touch with reality that your ideas don't deserve serious consideration. So, I'm just going to imbibe the idiocy for a few laughs." I received this an hour before class; she was reacting to a newspaper article I'd written that was critical of a community festival. Deeply hurt, I was *strongly* tempted to write a return scathing e-mail, but, instead, penned a brief reply stating that language/sentiment like she used does not foster constructive criticism, and asked if she would like to be removed from the mailing list for future articles. I felt better after transmitting the reply, but was still quite rattled. I asked myself if I should cancel class, and agonized for the better part of the hour before hitting on an intriguing idea: why don't I *use* the incident to illustrate the topic for the day? As it turned out, luck or providence or fate or whatever was with me as the topic—the sociological imagination (Mills 1959)—was an ideal framework for discussion.[2]

After a few announcements I apologized in advance for being "off," but explained that I was rattled by an unsettling e-mail that I'd read just before class. I briefly summarized its content and concluded that I'd do my best to try to minimize its effect on the day's performance. A few minutes later, though (after laying out the basics of the sociological imagination), I returned the e-mail to the table. Or, I should say, I put *my* reaction to the e-mail on display.

"Who are you to imply that I'm an idiot, you white bitch" was my initial reaction, a reaction I shared with the class—in explicit language. I added that I thought "you don't have a degree in sociology, so shut the fuck up about shit you got no clue about!" After a brief pause to let the imagery sink in, I informed the class that here I was *not* using the sociological imagination, that my classist, sexist, and racist initial thoughts were the product of unreflective reaction. I explained that the articulation—the connection of elements to serve a particular interest or idea—that I made was not necessary or natural and that we should try to figure out a different, more empowering articulation. For instance, we could either rationalize the reaction as somehow justified given my friend's personal shortcomings, or utilize critical thinking and try to figure out why she reacted the way she did *and* what was the rationale behind *my* responses. Among other things, I discussed our differential ideologies about capitalism, and the effects of our social structural positionings and resulting experiences/perspectives. This, I concluded, is using the sociological imagination.

It is important, I think, to note that I focused on my own shortcomings, rather than on my friend's, for (at least) two reasons. First, she was not there to defend herself, so out of fairness I minimized reflection on her and pointedly noted that I was only speculating about her perspectives. As argued by many [such as hooks (1994b, 1990), Johnson (1995), and Simon (1995)], we have to be extremely cautious in representing the Other. Second, by voicing our own shortcomings and fears, instructors help reduce distance between themselves and their students, and challenge traditional notions of teacher as infallible Author(ity). By sharing ourselves, *and* opening up for critical reflection, we not only give students an additional text to read that facilitates understandings of course material, we help them practice critical pedagogy's project of deconstructing authority and resisting passive acceptance of knowledge/truth claims. By deconstructing our articulations with the class, we help students make pertinent rearticulations for their own lives. At the heart of this project is what I call "the three EXs": exposure, explosion, and explication.

First, of course, is exposure. As instructors, one of our primary tasks is to introduce foreign concepts and experiences to our students. As part of this effort many teachers employ texts of everyday life, ranging from fictionalized accounts such as short stories to "factual" sources like newspaper articles. Teachers can also include personal experiences here, in an attempt of *both* teacher and student to gain new understandings. Henry Giroux (1994:133) argues that

As agents, students and others need to learn how to take risks, to understand how power works differently as both a productive and a dominating force, to be able to "read" the world from a variety of perspectives, and to be willing to think beyond the commonsense assumptions that govern everyday experience.

bell hooks (1994a:21) expands on the use of "risk" in exposure, arguing that empowerment cannot happen if teachers ask students to share what they would not share, and/or take risks that they would not take:

It is often productive if professors take the first risk, linking confessional narratives to academic discussions so as to show how experience can illuminate and enhance our understanding of academic material. But professors must practice being vulnerable in the classroom, being wholly present in mind, body, and spirit.

Such vulnerability is suggested by my second "ex": explosion. Giroux (1994) and hooks (1994a) argue that sharing confessionals can be done in such a way that *heightens* distance and reifies authority. For instance, if I had slightly edited my articulation of the elements evoked by the e-mail, I could very easily have constructed a scenario of WALT = sophisticated and cool/FRIEND (and, by extension, anyone who does not share teacher's knowledge/standpoint) = reactionary and temperamental. It is imperative, then, that teachers as text "explode" their narratives in such a way that dispels the artificial aspects of authority (it's not right just because we say it's right), and exhibits our humanness, demonstrating that we too are susceptible to various "isms" (classism, sexism, racism, etc.) and—just like students—struggle against compliance with systems of privilege. In the case with my friend, for instance, it was crucial that I highlight the operation of the patriarchy and bourgeois class consciousness in my use of sexist terms and disparaging thoughts about our differential educational obtainment; teachers need to explain that we are never fully "enlightened," nor do we ever effortlessly escape the pull of oppressive systems. According to Giroux (1996:136):

[T]hose who engage in education and cultural work must use [authority] critically to organize and analyze their own cultural work in order to be attentive to the politics of their own location institutionally but also to avoid committing pedagogical terrorism with their students. By allowing their own forms of authority to be held up to critical scrutiny, authority itself becomes an object of social analysis and can then be viewed as central to the conditions necessary for ownership and production of knowledge.

The second component of explosion overlaps with the third "ex": explication. After using our articulations of experiences to expose students to new ideas, and exploding—disarticulating—those perspectives into its constitutive parts, we then, finally, must demonstrate how everything fits together in larger systems of domination and oppression. Such an effort, furthermore, must be done in a way that does not reinforce those systems. I used the experience with my friend to illustrate the operation of race, that I, an African American, was capable of being racist. I used this articulation to facilitate a very open reflection by my predominately white class on racism. Of course, I stressed that all racisms are not equal; the key, though, to an honest examination was the dispersal of the "innocent black subject," the belief that African Americans exist outside of a corrupting aspect of raced power (Hall 1992; see also Haraway 1991). The class and I discussed how it is a much more difficult and perilous task to view race as a dynamic of shifting truths and falsehoods rather than a set of immutable determined facts (Omi and Winant 1994). After exposure to alternative narratives based on our own lived experiences, and explosion of those narratives into their constitutive parts, teachers must explicate new narratives that help teacher and student alike in the never-ending quest to create empowered, yet non-exploitative, subjectivities.

The teacher as text strategy means using ourselves in an effort to enable students to center themselves. Some would argue, however, that this inverts the professor–student relationship by placing authority in the students, as Long and Lake (1996) fear. Giroux (1996:179; see also West 1990) offers us a way to rethink "authority":

The issue for teachers is not to abandon judgements in the name of a false neutrality that suggests they simply be priests of an unproblematic truth; on the contrary, teachers and other cultural workers [and students] need to try to understand how the values that inform their work are historically conditioned and institutionally produced.

In doing so, "with a certain irony, when we actively adopt the authority of our positions in the classroom, this frees students to learn actively from each other and frees us to learn as actively from our students as they do from us" (O'Brien and Howard 1996:328). Keeping the three EXs in mind, in my classes I find that a willingness to explore my own vulnerabilities and complicities with oppressive systems, combined with a thorough knowledge of the subject material, go a long way toward establishing an open atmosphere in which students explore their *own* understandings, identities, and practices.

Before concluding this section, we should examine the larger institution within which I deploy this technique: the public university. The dominant model being increasingly applied to the pubic university is that of a corporation: it should become a leaner and trimmer operation, one that's more accountable to both owners (the citizens of the states) and students, the "customers" (Aronowitz 2000; Dellucchi and Korgen 2002; Kolodny 1998; Nelson 1997a, 1997b). One manifestation of this trend is students' expectations to be prepared with immediately marketable skills rather than to be taught the joys of learning for its own sake. Consider the thoughts of Prashad (1997:249):

The contemporary university is no longer a cloister to which the youth retire to "play" with ideas away from the cares of the world; these few postadolescent days cannot be spent without an eye to the prospects of each student in a world in which the gains of increased productivity (due to technology) have been monopolized by transnational corporations.

Like it or not, teachers are being forced to pay greater attention to the pressures of the market, even those (like me) who view the university as a site of contestation and instability, where the goal is to foster an environment "in which a spectrum of plausible ideas come into play, so that class members—as well as the person deemed the 'teacher'—might enter a collective experience to sort out things anew each term" (Wald 1997:133). This does not, however, mean that it is my job to police politically correct thought in a class as Pensieve, manipulating ideas of desirable social and spatial utopias. This is what Giroux (1996:127) calls "politicizing education," which "silences in the name of a specious universalism and denounces all transformative practices through an appeal to a timeless notion of truth and beauty." No, we must adopt "political education," which decenters power, and calls attention to and critiques efforts to unjustly stratify groups and reify inequality: "Politicizing education perpetuates pedagogical violence, while a political education expands the pedagogical conditions for students to understand how power works on them, through them, and for them in the service of constructing and deepening their roles as engaged thinkers and critical citizens" (Giroux 1996:53).

Teachers must, in other words, offer our own value systems—which structure the very nature of the class—for analysis: we set the ground rules, but stress that even these can be challenged; teachers and students both investigate implications of various challenges. Teachers provide maps of political and/or politicized social terrain to help students negotiate various social worlds (O'Shea 1998); we help students figure out what they may encounter on journeys, but it's up to them to figure out which direction to take once they consider the possibilities.

hooks (1994a) argues that a certain amount of resistance to this project is desirable, as it indicates that we are really challenging deeply held (yet often un or underanalyzed) convictions. She writes that we must teach students that "joy can be present *along with hard work*. . . . And sometimes it's necessary to remind students and colleagues that pain and painful situations don't necessarily translate into harm. We make that very fundamental mistake all the time. Not all pain is harm, and not all pleasure is good" [Ron Scapp, in a conversation with bell hooks (1994a:154; emphasis in original)]. According to Takata (1997:200), "learning is messy. . . . There are often frustrating detours, temporary setbacks, and latent learning," but adopting the teacher as text position is one method of alleviating this form of resistance. By "emphasiz[ing] the partiality of any approach to challenging oppression and the need to constantly rework these approaches" (Kumashiro 2001:4), and by demonstrating that teachers are as deeply immersed in the complex muck as are the students—yet somehow manage to survive and, indeed, thrive in chaotic and disorienting spaces—teachers can help instill a sense of hope in students and encourage them to tackle tough questions.

In essence, teachers as text construct themselves as heuristics, aiding students in their projects of discovery and recreation of their subjectivities. In a postmodern era in which it is said that we have fluid identities that are continually subject to reinterpretation and reinscription in the wake of such globally influenced and influencing socializing agents as the electronic media (Kellner 2003, 1995a; Sholle and Denski 1993) and consumer culture (Jameson 1983; Lury 1996), teachers as text attempt to help their students make sense of ever-fluctuating and ubiquitous images and representations of who we were, are, and should be. A teacher as text says that "this is how it is for me, use my experiences as a guide to help figure out how it is for you." In a world in which information about information is a crucial component of the critical imagination, the teacher as text may be an invaluable resource.

There are, of course, many other very powerful strategies for creating heuristics. Few, however, place the teacher so centrally in the process as the teacher as text project. For instance, techniques in journals like *Teaching Sociology* usually concern "icebreaker" activities to be done in the first week of classes. The teacher as text, in contrast, is employed throughout the semester. In fact, the technique often requires time and repeated exposure to take full effect, as suggested by this evaluation from a white male student in a "race and ethnic relations" class: "When I first walked in the class, I thought 'Oh no, this black man is going to talk about nothing but racism and how the Man keeps him down.' Your stories like the bike stop made me realize that it's more complex." The student was referring to a midterm discussion of how I was stopped by a police officer while riding my bike at midnight because I "fit the description" of a known perpetrator (an African American man who rides a bicycle at night!). I told the class how I—during the stop—was initially excited to get lived experience of possible discrimination that I could share with the class, but then became concerned that I might be taken to the station on the officer's whim. We discussed how as a privileged academic I could enjoy parts of the experience, but as an African American might be concerned about racist treatment. Later, we added other social locations to the matrix, discussing, among other things, gendered harassment to which men would generally be immune (e.g., I wouldn't think twice about wandering around at midnight). Note that "not just any partial perspective will do; we must be hostile to easy relativisms and holisms built out of summing and subsuming parts" (Haraway 1991:192). The standpoints of the subjugated are not "innocent," and must be examined, decoded, and interpreted, just like the standpoints of the privileged. This is Collins's (1991) matrix of domination: we must illustrate the operation of both privileged and dominated identities and resulting experiences, and be willing to explore their intersections instead of selecting the most convenient (justification of a simplistic right/wrong) understanding.

hooks (1994a:11) argues that "Teaching is a performative act. . . . Teachers are not performers in the traditional sense of the word in that our work is not meant to be a spectacle. Yet it is meant to serve as a catalyst that calls everyone to become more and more engaged, to become active participants in learning." Students are invited to participate in a "radical democracy" in which they use various texts (including the media) to critically engage the world, learning how power is deployed and creates both affective and cognitive investment:

Radical democracy in this context serves as a critical referent for analyzing how the conditions of democratic life have been eroded through a market culture and bureaucratic state in which access to power and pleasure is limited to few groups wielding massive amounts of economic and political power while being relatively unaccountable to those groups below them. (Giroux 1996:134)

In my classes I share my personal experiences with the students in an attempt to practice radical democracy and political education. I use these experiences to illustrate theoretical concepts, and encourage the students to use my articulation to understand how power works both productively and destructively in their own lived experience. In the next, concluding, section of this chapter I discuss the framework in which I first used autoethnography to simultaneously deploy this "teacher as text" strategy and record its successes and failures.

The Autoethnography of Sociology s101

The ways that mass cultural images pervade style and fashion suggest that cultural identity is constituted in part by iconic images of ethnic cultural heroes, which are badges of identity and forces of division between the races [and genders, classes, sexual orientations, etc.]. . . . Media culture also provides modern morality tales that demonstrate right and wrong behavior, that show what to do and what not to do, that indicate what is or is not "the right thing."

A media culture has emerged in which images, sounds, and spectacles help produce the fabric of everyday life, dominating leisure time, shaping political views and social

behavior, and providing the materials out of which people forge their very identities. . . .
Media stories and images provide the symbols, myths, and resources which help consti-
tute a common culture for the majority of individuals in many parts of the world today.

These are the epigraphs on the syllabi for my sociology classes of fall
1997 and spring 1998. Both are from Douglas Kellner's (1995a) *Media*
Culture, but they were used in slightly different ways. The first passage
comes from page 162 and was used on the fall syllabus. The title of that
class was "media in society," therefore I had to have a somewhat broad
interpretation of "media," covering institutional as well as semiotic aspects. The passage from the fall syllabus privileges mass-market production of normality and morality. The second passage, on the other
hand, is taken from page 1 and is more concerned with the operation of
identities and semiotic aspects of culture, which is more appropriate for
a class entitled "media culture." This is not to say that this class ignored
larger institutional determinants of "culture"; both classes were concerned with the tension between two understandings of culture as a
"whole way of life" and the "production and circulation of meaning"
(du Gay et al. 1997).

Indeed, that tension is central to the "circuit of culture," which is a
focal point of many of my other classes as well as the media classes. Du
Gay and colleagues (1997) argue that to thoroughly understand cultural practices, texts, and artifacts we must study their representation,
identities, production, consumption, and regulation, and the interactions among these five terms. In the 1997–1998 classes I used *Doing Cul-*
tural Studies as a textbook to illustrate the circuit of culture for one
product—the Sony Walkman—and applied the concept to all other
texts introduced and studied. I maintained the resulting tension
between the two understandings of culture throughout each class in an
attempt to engage students in the subtle nuances of the interaction of
their personal biographies and institutional structures.

Despite the minor variation in course names and course content,
both classes were essentially "media and society" classes, focusing on
the development of "critical media literacy," which I define as the ability to simultaneously enjoy media and media products while being rig-
orously analytical about the information and understandings we draw
from words, images, and sounds. The objectives of both courses (listed
on the syllabi) were to:

- Construct an historical overview of media in U.S.society, along with
  comparisons with developments around the globe.
- Gain a basic understanding of key concepts used in the study of
  media in society.

- Become aware that media contribute to the creation and maintenance of social inequalities in the United States, and that we all contribute to this system of oppression and domination on various levels.
- Construct a cultural studies theoretical framework (which encompasses insights from Sociology, Communications, English, Comparative Literature, History, and Philosophy) from which we will investigate contemporary social issues as constructed and/or reported through the media.
- Investigate ways in which we can use this cultural studies perspective in the struggle to create more democratic and humane societies. We will learn to resist the influences of oppressive ideologies and work toward creating a better society for ourselves as individuals, as members of social collectivities, and as participants in American society.

To accomplish these goals my classes usually use an electronic classroom, two essays, and a final project. Following are descriptions of each of these components (as well as a media journal) as they appeared on the 1997–1998 syllabi:

- *Electronic Classroom.* It is impossible to cover the entire field of media and society in one course. In an attempt to touch on as many aspects as possible, we will participate in an electronic classroom (EC) where we will (1) expand on themes raised in the lecture setting and (2) explore new avenues that are not formally addressed in the physical classroom. Students are required to post at least one message per week (by Sunday at 6:00 P.M.) in one of the three discussion areas of the EC: the "coffee house," in which you can talk about any issue or event, as long as it is related to the media in some way; the "debate house," in which an assistant will post a question about media and society with a request for pro/con debate on that question; or the "reflect house," in which you will be asked to visit an Internet site and discuss your reactions to the site and how it affects (or doesn't) your perspectives, identities, and behaviors. You can choose a different house each week, or post messages in more than one house per week, but you must *post at least one message in one of the houses per week*. These postings will be graded on a +/- (complete/incomplete) basis.
- *Media Journal.* As previously noted, a key objective will be the development of critical media literacy. To accomplish this goal, you will compile a journal of your encounters with media culture, and how your interpretation of event/issues was affected by current

understandings of the operation of media culture, and how you think those encounters were affected by external events. You will make at least one entry per week. Each entry will have the following three components: (1) description of media product/text, (2) your interpretation of that product/text, and (3) influence of outside activities/events/reflections. For example, one week you may (1) describe an episode of *Seinfeld* that you found fascinating, (2) provide your interpretation that while Jerry's comments about Native Americans were insensitive, they were not racist, and (3) talk about how after our class discussion of racism in the media you would have termed the depiction racist, but after a talk with your Native American roommate your views shifted somewhat. I will collect the journals at midterm to check your progress and issue suggestions for improvement. These journals will be private and will only be read and graded by the instructor.

- *Essays.* Establishing connections between theoretical material and lived experience will be critical to our efforts. In the two essay papers we will use the sociological imagination to create linkages between material explored in class, contemporary public issues, and our own personal thoughts, feelings, and understandings. Essay guidelines will be provided with each individual assignment. Late papers will not be accepted.
- *Term Paper.* Throughout the course we learn that there are a number of different ideas and perspectives based on our social locations (race, ethnicity, class, gender, sexual orientation, etc.) and intra and intergroup experiences. In the final paper we will utilize the techniques explored throughout the course in an exploration of cross-group mediated communication and understanding. Each student will be required to analyze a media cultural text (a movie, TV show, musical recording, series of advertisements, etc.) with at least one other person [who differs from you in at least two ways with regard to gender, race, ethnicity, class, and sexual orientation (and who does not necessarily have to be a member of the class)], in order to examine relationships between media images and the actual experience of multigroup contact and interaction. More detailed information will be passed out after midterm.

The EC instructions allude to one of the duties of my undergraduate teaching assistants (TAs). I use undergraduate TAs in most of my classes because they are priceless learning resources for enrolled students, and the experience is rewarding for the TAs themselves (Jacobs 2002; see also chapter 6). During the 1997–1998 media culture classes the TAs also served as research assistants in autoethnographically creating and studying the classes as Pensieves. In addition to one-on-one attention and experience in a large-scale research project, the undergraduates received course credit for participation. I selected three students to work with me during the full year, and they earned six hours of credit (three each semester) for sociology s494 ("field research in sociology"). Thus, I named them "the 494 crew."[3]

Each member of the 494 crew had been a student in my s335 "race and ethnic relations" course (though from different semesters), and each received an A in the course. They were also all interested in graduate school (sociology as well as other possibilities), so getting a taste of sociological research was useful for them. I also wanted a diverse group in order to maximize (auto)ethnographic scope and power, and achieved that, as will be detailed in subsequent chapters.

Lori Canada is white, a single mother, working class, bisexual, and three to four years older than most of the other students. More important than just possessing several subaltern identities, Lori constantly evaluates what these identities mean, in and of themselves, and how they fit together. She was a participant in two of my race and ethnicity classes, first as a student and then as my very first TA. She was used to my "teacher as text" project and—most important—willing to speak up and challenge me when necessary, thereby adding another level to the project's heuristic: authority can and should be challenged in an effort to figure out how it can and does work in other contexts, and how challenges may be received and negotiated.

Beeta Homaifar is Iranian American, upper middle class, and a double major in economics and sociology. As was the case with Lori, the articulation of these (and other) identities is more important than the identities themselves.[4] Beeta was perceived as the most "normal" of the assistants, so she shared the closest bond with students, eliciting thoughts about many subjects, class and nonclass related alike. Additionally, Beeta's field notes were consistently full of needed foundational observations and minute descriptions of class interactions. A detailed description and discussion of "what happened" are essential to a good ethnography (Corsaro 1985; Van Maanen 1986).

Robert Perez is Mexican American, working class, and very sympathetic to Marxist analysis. As were Lori and Beeta, he was in one of my previous race and ethnic relations courses, and stood out as one of the few who consistently questioned received wisdom from the beginning of class. In fact, Rob questions the project of "autoethnography" itself—preferring "Chicago school" ethnographies, such as Anderson's (1990) *Streetwise* and Duneier's (1992) *Slim's Table*—and, thus, provided ongoing productive methodological critique. We'll see examples of this later, particularly in chapter 4.

The 494 crew came to each fall semester class, took ethnographic notes [using Corsaro's (1985) field note scheme], typed up those notes, and posted them to an electronic classroom for review (this EC was accessible only by the four of us). We met each Friday to discuss concerns with all aspects of the project, such as methodological problems and suggestions for future approaches. During the spring semester they did not attend any classes; we met periodically to develop analyses of our experiences.

In addition to the three members of the 494 crew, I employed two other undergraduate students as assistants. During the fall semester Anna Lindzy was enrolled in the class. Anna was a student in a previous "race and ethnic relations" class, and received an A. In lieu of doing the essays and final project, I asked her to keep an "unofficial" ethnography of class dynamics (she also compiled a media journal). This ethnography is "unofficial" in that I just threw her into the mix with no instruction on how to do ethnography. I will include some of her perspectives in later chapters.

Jennifer Richie was also a student in the fall class. During the spring semester she served as the undergraduate teaching assistant, and was also the research assistant for a 1998–1999 focus group extension (see chapter 6) of the 1997–1998 classroom autoethnography. Her duties as the spring semester TA were to run the EC's "debate house" and to take ethnographic notes in the manner of the 494 crew of the fall semester. I gave her more training than Anna but not as much as the 494 crew (I gave Jennifer a copy of my guide to field notes and a copy of my field notes from the first day of the fall class). Although the assistants received different levels of training and, subsequently, produced different types of data, all data were extremely valuable to the overarching project. We will gain a sharper picture of Jennifer (as well as the others) in future chapters.

I will also provide biographical data on myself as part of the next chapter. In a sense, such biographical data (as well as that of the assistants) is as essential as direct observation, since the foundation of an autoethnography of a Pensieve is reflexively interrogating the effects of social positionings and experiences. In this project we learn how "dominator culture has tried to keep us all afraid, to make us choose safety instead of risk, sameness instead of diversity. Moving through that fear, finding out what connects us, reveling in our differences; this is the process that brings is closer, that gives us a world of shared values, of meaningful community" (hooks 2003:197).

Chapter Three

Fragments of the Sociological Imagination

Cultural studies is part of a critical media pedagogy that enables individuals to resist media manipulation and increase their freedom and individuality. It can empower people to gain sovereignty over their culture and enable them to struggle for alternative cultures and political change. Cultural studies is not just another academic fad but can be part of a better society and a better life.

—DOUGLAS KELLNER,
"Cultural Studies, Multiculturalism, and Media Culture"

The sociological imagination enables its possessor to understand the larger historical scene in terms of its meaning for the inner life and the external career of a variety of individuals. . . . [It] enables us to grasp history and biography and the relations between the two within society. . . . [It] is the capacity to shift from one perspective to another . . . to range from the most impersonal and remote transformations to the most intimate features of the human self—and to see the relations between the two.

—C. WRIGHT MILLS, *The Sociological Imagination*

My task as a sociologist is to teach my students the sociological imagination as applicable to late modern/postmodern American society. This means incorporating elements of the cultural studies project as described by Kellner, as America becomes an increasingly electronically mediated society where "we can no longer think of the media as providing secondary representations of reality; they affect and produce the reality that they mediate. We live in a world of media events and media realities" (Fiske 1994a:xv). While stopping short of attempting to enter a "hyperreality" where social and cultural simulations are more "real" than the material products and conditions on which they are based (Baudrillard 1994, 1986), I try to teach my students that life in America's immense electronic media culture means that our perceptions of life are, for better or worse, intricately intertwined with representations in TV, movies, books, newspapers, music, and advertisements. As Goldfarb (2002:7) notes, "engagement in media technology and its institutions is not a choice but an inevitability of life in a . . . culture shaped by an ethos of the visual and of media pedagogy." In classrooms as Pensieves students and instructors learn to make the best of this situation, using their sociological imaginations to juxtapose multiple fragments of lived experience in empowering ways.

I jump into this project right away, on the first day of each semester. As the students enter the classroom I ask them to pick up a syllabus, instructions for accessing the electronic classroom, and an index card. On the index cards I usually ask for their name, e-mail, year and major, reason for taking the class, and favorite recent commercial (or movie). After allowing students sufficient time to browse the materials, I share my own answers to the index card questions, present an overview of the course, and go through the syllabus.

I tell each class that I will answer the index card questions in an effort to help them get to know me right away and to obtain a sense of what the course will be like. I tell each class to call me Walt, not Dr. Jacobs or professor or anything like that. This is done as part of my overall effort to decrease the artificial, unnecessary aspects of the hierarchical student–teacher relationship (hooks 1994a).

I then usually describe how I became a sociology professor, warning them that it's not a straightforward story. I majored in Electrical Engineering as an undergraduate at the Georgia Institute of Technology, and my first and only postgraduation engineering job took me from the metropolis of Atlanta, Georgia, to a Department of Defense facility in rural south-central Indiana. I expected and was prepared for the drastic change in the racial composition of my environment, but was stunned to find that I was truly an Other in the workplace: in a building of hundreds I was one of the very few African Americans, urbanites, Democrats, pro-feminists, non-Christians, etc., etc. Aside from gender and sexual orientation (and possibly social class, depending on its operationalization) I was quite the standout.

During my first year at this facility, however, things went smoothly, as both my co-workers and I were intrigued by how well we got along, given that our social locations and experiences were so very different. I even designed a few "surveys" to try to figure out what was going on; one of my graduate school professors says that I was doing "sociology without a license." When mutual curiosity and openness between my co-workers and I turned to wariness and attempts at proselytization I decided to discover if I could get the license.

I also usually tell the students about how those experiences were explicitly revisited in my graduate school master's thesis, in which I conducted in-depth interviews with twelve of my former co-workers to explore our past interactions and their perceptions of me as a person who attempted to improve race relations between blacks and whites. That experience, in turn, has influenced my teaching philosophy and methods employed throughout graduate school and as a professor.

During the 1997–1998 autoethnography of my "media and society" classes I told each group of students that the class would be very different from those of many other sociology instructors who regarded the syllabus as a set contract that includes a clause stating that the syllabus would not be changed (and that student should drop the class if the student didn't agree with everything in it). In my classes the syllabus is a map of possible routes to take: the course is an exploration of new social worlds, and students should feel free to take risks and experiment with new ideas and perspectives, challenging them as well as me, the instructor. As part of this effort I can't say exactly what we'd do and where we'd end up, therefore I would never establish my syllabus as an unchangeable contract. During the autoethnography I concluded the course overview by informing the students that other sections of the course were available if my setup was too weird. I did, however, encourage everyone to stay and experience my approach, even if unusual.[1] I told the students that we would co-create pedagogical tools and experiences, as "ultimately, the classroom is always a site of intercultural communication. It is a border crossing where the culturally and racially lived experiences of teachers and students become tender for negotiation" (Alexander 1999:328).

In the second week of the fall class of the autoethnography, and the third week of the spring class (the second week was cut short due to the MLK holiday), I asked the students to anonymously give me their impressions of the first day of class. Here are a few of their responses:

At first I thought that the class was going to be boring because I didn't really know what it was like. When you walked in the room the first thing I noticed was that you were drinking a Fruitopia and wearing a "Basketball is Life" [T-shirt]. I knew at that point that the class wouldn't be boring because the instructor looked like he had a personality. (fall response)

I just felt like some people aren't going to take this class seriously like they should. I think the semester will be a very interesting one . . . if people keep an "open mind". . . . (fall response)

I was a little intimidated when I first came into class, it's a large class. I was glad that Walt was African-American, because I don't think IU has enough professors of different races. (fall response)

I had a great first impression of this class. You immediately caught my attention and the subject matter seemed interesting. The only part I didn't like was the fact that the grade is based on papers, which I hate to write. (spring response)

I was disappointed after the first day and considered dropping the course. I think I was mostly uncomfortable with having such a large discussion group. . . . After 2 weeks, I am glad I hung in there, I'm a little more comfortable and hope to learn a lot. (spring response)

I was impressed at the level of comfort the teacher has in front of the class—I mean how he tries to make things interesting, and feeling at ease. (spring response)

When I came into this classroom I was impressed with the music. I guess that this is the first thing that hit me. For an instructor to play music, that's cool, but jazz? Real cool. (spring response)

Cool, he's not old school, he seems really cool/original/different. (spring response)

I told the students that some of the things they might consider putting in the first impressions were reactions to my race, the use of music, and my age. As their responses show (along with a vast majority of uncited ones), the students liked the fact that I played music (usually jazz) at the beginning of each class to establish a relaxed mood, though a few were worried that this made things too relaxed. Most, also, were comfortable with my age (twenty-nine at the time) and race, and a few cited these as positives that would add to the benefits they expected to extract from the course. I will discuss these "teacher as text" dynamics in more detail, first in the analysis of the results of a fragment from the movie *I Like It Like That* (Martin 1994), then class reactions to an advertisement by the Gap, and finally in an analysis of postings (concerning exposure to fragments from musical sources) in the electronic classroom. Overall, though nervous and unsure about exactly what was to come, students in both semesters reported that they were excited and anxious to begin the journey.

Screening *I Like It Like That*

An old fashioned tale is told with a few modern twists in this family drama, set primarily in the racially blended 167th block of the Bronx. The street is filled with many people. Tensions can run high and occasionally erupt into violence. Recently a slain cop was memorialized on a neighborhood mural. The late cop was Chino's brother. Chino is concerned with his machismo and even times himself, as he has sex with Lisette, his wife. Other than sack time, the two lead a hectic family life. Not only do they have three wild children of their own, they must also deal with Lisette's brother who wants to be a transsexual, and with Rosaria, Chino's nit-picky mother. In addition they are always embroiled with financial problems. Chino is still being pursued by Magdalena, who may have borne his child. Chino is thrown in jail after stealing during a black-out. Lisette, to pay his bail, ends up as an assistant to record label executive Stephen Price. After hearing a rumor that Lisette has become involved with Price, Chino begins an affair with Magdalene upon his release. The children suffer from the actions of their parents. (plot synopsis from "The All-Movie Guide" web site)

I Like It Like That is a 1994 movie written and directed by Darnell Martin (1994). The movie received the 1994 New York Film Critics' Circle awards for best new director and best first film, and was nominated for best first feature, best actor, and best actress 1995 Independent Spirit awards. During both semesters of the autoethnography I showed the class a seven-minute clip from the movie. In the clip the Puerto Rican Lisette is attempting to win a job with Price, a white executive with few ties to communities of color. Price is trying to sign two Puerto Rican brothers to his record label, and wants a beautiful Puerto Rican woman posing as his assistant to demonstrate that he is "down," that he knows Puerto Rican culture and respects its people. Lisette is sent over by Price's real assistant and when she doesn't measure up to his standards of beauty, Price tries to dismiss her. She stays and shares ideas about how to improve the band's image, which the band loves. Price quickly falls into line and praises her and her ideas too—until the brothers depart, at which time he tries to get rid of her again. She "hustles" him for a ride home ("How about I call Ricky and tell him I'm not really your assistant?") and, on the way, demonstrates once again that her lived cultural experience can be an invaluable business asset: upon listening to a demo tape of another group that Price wants to sign she informs him that they were not received well at a party in the Bronx, home of Price's target audience: young urban people of color.

I showed this clip twice to the spring class and three times to the fall class, in order to measure the ways in which student critical literacy changed (or did not) over time. The fall class saw the clip during weeks 1 (on the second day overall), 8, and 15. The spring class screened the clip during weeks 2 (on the third day overall) and 7. I did not screen the clip a third time in the spring for three reasons: (1) in the fall several students expressed annoyance over having to watch the same text on three different occasions; (2) in the fall there was not much change in reception from the second to third readings (as opposed to considerable change from the first to second), and I had indications that the pattern would be the same in the spring; and (3) I did not really need a third reading since I changed the purpose of multiple readings of the clip from an attempt to gauge "how much" critical literacy changed to "what ways" it evolved.

In each class I called attention to political economic situation, textual analysis, and ethnographic reception issues of the text. I'll discuss textual analysis and ethnographic reception issues as part of the "teacher as text" strategy later; as for political economic situation I analyzed the movie's setting in multi-ethnic New York City and the time frame of its production (with a multiracial cast and crew) in 1993–1994, and compared that with our 1997–1998 existence in rural Indiana, at a state university that is 85 percent white. I introduced (during the first screenings) or recalled (subsequent screenings) the notion of "hegemony," that students' understandings are the result of struggle within unevenly occupied terrain of struggle in which some groups have more power to construct favorable representations of themselves and unfavorable accounts of others, and that these social constructions have very real material and cultural effects beyond the personal (Fiske 1994a; Giroux 1994, 1996; Kellner 2003, 1995a, 1995b). I called attention to the United States as a hegemonic society, wherein articulations about who and what our society was, is, and should be are subject to continual debate, on an uneven playing field.

My task, again, was to help the students create powerful sociological imaginations, to investigate implications of their articulations of personal biographical experiences and social structural issues. One of my fall field notes (October 28) summarizes the two major ways in which this was developed between the first and second readings of the clip:

Read second set of responses to I Like It Like That. About half of class had different reactions. Issues:

1. A few more critical because "Knew what was coming" and focused on details. This is unavoidable artifact of method.
2. A few women (especially Brenda)[2] noticed gender more, perhaps because less afraid to be "feminist."
3. A number indicated that they had strong reactions first time, but didn't fully understand them. Now they think they have better grasp.

4. Matrix of domination in operation. Most significant difference: notice ethnicity this time. To be expected, as most are White.

So, then, 2 interlocking issues here, illustrating critical literacy:

   a. Better sense of existing perception (3 and 1).
   b. Formed new interpretations (4 and 2).

Brenda, for instance, writes that "I didn't notice the 'objectification of women' the first time, but I did this time. . . . I'm not a psycho-feminist or anything, but (through Walt's encouragement to step back and look at things with a sociological imagination) I could see the issue of gender more clearly this time." I think that Brenda's "psycho" means "shrill and obsessed." In her media journal she wrote that "I'm not some feminist who looks for instances where women are slighted!!" She prefers to call herself a "modern woman."

I will identify other individual students (from both fall and spring semesters) by pseudonym and examine their reactions to *I Like It Like That*—along with other products like journal entries and EC postings—in the "spotlight" boxes of this chapter and chapters 4–6; the spotlight for "Nate" follows this section. A general compilation of fall semester students' reactions to the second viewing of *I Like It Like That* includes:

- After seeing the clip again, I can detect bias even more.
- I watched the segment this time much more critically.
- This time, the class differences stood out to me more.
- I didn't even notice that he got a Latino girl to talk to his Latino friends.
- [Price] was trying to appeal to the Menedez's ethnicity to get them signed.
- First time I saw it, I thought it was trying to show that minorities are poor and live in slums and the women minorities are all prostitutes. [This time] I thought more about how women in general are portrayed.
- I still see the characters as stereotypes. But now it's because of the images and ideas society implicates on us.
- I basically had the same critical reaction as last time I watched the clip. However, I feel that I now have a better understanding of my reaction.

Concerning students whose reactions didn't change much, this is to be expected, and, to a degree, is encouraging, as resistance to changes in critical thought can indicate that deeply help convictions are indeed being challenged (hooks 1994a). As an outspoken feminist, for instance, Jennifer had a very strong reaction to gender roles in the clip: "To be honest, my reactions are not much different from last time because I already was viewing the clip extraordinarily critically. I might have loosened up a bit from last time, because I really did try to enjoy it. However, I haven't diverted much from my original position." Even after I encouraged her to further enter the matrix of domination (Collins 1991) and look at intersections with other categorizations, in the third reading Jennifer still privileged gender. This, though, is an instance of resistance that's grounded in a principled stand as opposed to ambivalence or unreflective reaction.

The spring class also had its mixture of critical consideration and apathy. As in the fall, the responses that expressed the conviction that they were more critical readers were that they (a) had a better sense of existing perceptions, or (b) formed new interpretations. There was an important difference, however. The spring responses were much more likely to be of type (a) than of type (b), whereas the opposite was more prominent in the fall. This is due to the spring class being positioned differently than the fall class (predominantly juniors and seniors in the spring; mostly freshmen and sophomores in the fall), so they were both able to voice and were more experienced in making sociological articulations, even if they didn't know they were doing so.[3] The spring class, then, was able to sharpen existing articulations while naming them and the specific processes involved:

- There is not much of a change from last time except that I can use certain terminology to describe what I see.
- I think this film is trying to make a point about cross-cultural (or subcultural) relations.
- Music seems to say a lot about a culture, and the different types of music show how different and diverse groups of people are.
- Since last time I have realized the intertextuality which I brought to the table when watching this.
- Since the last time I viewed the clip, it is clear that I am able to notice many of the concepts that we have covered thus far in class. . . . It allowed me to view the clip in a 'different' way, and appreciate it on a different level.
- I picked up many of the cultural and sociological nuances before, but I was a little more critical this time because I was looking at the media's biases more seriously than before, where I simply found it humorous.

- I still think stereotypes are shown, but added the matrix [of domination].

As can be expected, the spring class provided more complicated textual and experiential analyses during the brief discussion after the first screening (on subsequent occasions I just collected their data and moved on to different topics). For instance, when I announced that "two of my Puerto Rican friends said the portrayal was very realistic" a student reminded us that this doesn't necessarily mean the story *is* realistic; I had to articulate this myself in the fall: authenticity claims by some members of a social group are often challenged by other members.

Overall, then, in one sense the critical literacy of the fall class increased "more," as they were the more inexperienced (academically) class, and, thus, had more to grasp and learn. Indeed, that finding is not much of a surprise. In another sense, however, while both classes exhibited more critical literacy, two different forms turned up: some students formed new interpretations of the workings of their social worlds, while others created sharper understandings of existing perceptions. In other words, some students formed a sociological imagination from scratch whereas others modified existing sociological imaginations. This complicates McLaughlin's (1996:153) claim that students have "lived the postmodern, and are adept at reading its artifacts." When students are not adept at reading media culture, they must be repeatedly exposed to the same texts and techniques—with subtle variation to reinforce old lessons and stimulate new connections. A fine line must be walked between boring students with "old" information (and, thus, risking that they will lose interest and attention) and an underexposure that leaves students with only a superficial gloss of complicated material. I will demonstrate how to walk this line in the remaining two sections of this chapter (and throughout later chapters as well, especially in chapter 4).

Nate—"successful" intervention

[Critical reactions have changed since viewing #2], but mainly because of other things that I have witnessed outside of this classroom in my years of life. At first I was looking for things about this class in it, but now I realize that everything from this class must come from one's experience outside of it. I just now realized this!! Thanks.

—NATE ON THE THIRD READING
(change in critical reactions from last viewing) of *I Like it Like That*

At a glance, it appears that I've made a mistake in assigning Nate—a sopho-more from the fall class—to the category of "successful" interventions, those students who learned to be more critical consumers of electronic media culture. After all, he says that his reactions have changed mostly from lessons learned outside the classroom. Taking a second look, however, sug-gests that Nate may have been one of my *most* successful interventions, as he's truly developed a sociological imagination of connecting his personal biography and experiences with understandings of larger social issues. The class provided him with the tools for creating sociological articulations, and afforded him a space to practice making those connections.

As noted in the preceding section, one of the reasons I didn't have the spring class view the *I Like It Like That* clip a third time was because few of the fall students' reactions changed much from viewings two to three. Nate was one of the few. Let's look at his progression:

Men using women, whites using minorities, in both respects—her and the two guys. People use others in society to get what they want. (first reading, critical reactions; had not seen the movie before)

The guy is a major prick and is just trying to get the two men to sign with his record company so he can make money off of them. He is also trying to use the latino girl to get what he wants, but this is basically seen as a bad social "game" because the white is the one that is in control. (second reading, critical reactions)

I didn't really see a difference from last time, except that I already knew what was going to happen!!! (second reading, change in critical reactions from last viewing)

I find this very much about the fact that women can really take control of their own destiny no matter how big of an asshole the male is (or race). (third reading, change in critical reactions from last time)

Although I would have liked to have seen an explicit connection with struc-tural forces in Nate's narrative of the third reading, it was heartening to see Nate including the possibility of empowerment in his discussion. Through-out most of the semester he focused on a cynical articulation of society, as indicated by the first and second readings, and exemplified by this week 2 EC posting:

This accident that took Princess Di's life is or should be a wake up call for everyone in the world. First of all they wouldn't be trying to get these pictures if all of society wouldn't pay for them. In my eyes anybody that buys these ridiculous newspapers [tabloids] is to blame just as much as the people who get paid to take the pictures. People these days don't need to know what kind of freakin' underwear or whatever someone that is in the public eye is wearing. It is none of their business.

Nate's other five EC postings similarly focused on the exploitative side of media. Most of the other fall students' postings were usually positive in tone. I think that Nate took more than a little pride in believing himself to be one of the few students who was not seduced by powerful media messages. Even though there were many other students who resisted the media in some (or many) ways, an early (September 30) coffee house posting illustrates an aspect in which Nate did stand out from his colleagues:

I am using this space to ponder why you (walt) are so into jazz, but yet never mention the greatest music of all ... BLUES!!!!!!!!!!!!!!!! In my eyes there is a very important social aura that has always surrounded the blues such as Robert Johnson, Muddy Waters, Howling Wolf, and the list goes on and on and on.... these greats were never recognized for being the talents that they were for one reason, their race. If one were to watch tv, nowadays they would see the great John Lee Hooker, BB King, Bo Diddley and Chuck Berry in Pepsi commercials all the way to Nike commercials. I have a hard time swallowing it personally. These people created rock and roll and NOW people notice. I wish that I had enough money to give these legends so that they would not need these rampant business swines to grossly use their heritage and music to make their own living, excuse me but this is sickening!! to me.

While a few students questioned my techniques with me privately, and a few more students complained about things with the 494 crew, Nate was the only fall student to publicly post a personal criticism. Indeed, although the comment was very mild, it is significant in that I did not stifle his voice. Additionally, he told Lori that my class was the only one he felt comfortable voicing criticisms of the teacher to the teacher (Lori FN, October 29).

When I ran into Nate in the spring he informed me that because of the class he decided to become a sociology major. This, of course, is one of the highest compliments a student can pay me. It is especially rewarding given that Nate earned a "B-" in the class; other students who've told me that they switched to sociology after my class all earned an "A." The major reason Nate received the grade, however, was that he did not complete half of his EC postings and several of his media journal entries. When he did apply himself he exhibited signs of a nice sociological imagination.

Nate did his final project on the movie *Kids in the Hall: Brain Candy*. In the concluding paragraph he notes that "In conclusion this was a good assignment for me. It helped me realize yet again that I am not going to end up agreeing with too many people. Even ones that I am close to, and especially when they are different socially than me." Toward the end of the semester Nate began to realize *why* he disagreed with others, and his in-class comments became less cynical, as he searched for ways to explore positive manifestations of difference (that is one of the reasons he decided to become a sociology major). I believe that the class provided him with a few tools to help in that process.

Race-ing "the Gap"

I sometimes felt like I was trying to find meaning that wasn't there. (fall course evaluation)

Expand horizons to talk less about racial issues and more about other issues. (spring course evaluation)

I also thought it would be good to have an African-American male instructor to see how his opinions and viewpoints about the media compare and contrast with mine. (spring first impression)

The "teacher as text" strategy involves sharing my experiences and understandings of my social locations in an effort to help students better comprehend their own perspectives and the implications of creating some articulations and not others. My most visible positioning was race, and I tried to complicate student understandings of this slippery concept. As illustrated by the comment on the spring "first impressions" assignment, some students grasped this process and viewed it positively, whereas others thought I spent too much time on it, that it was an obsession. As will be explored in chapter 4 with the text *Space Traders*, this is to be expected when a predominantly white class is taught by an African American instructor, that they'll desire to downplay its significance, and accuse the instructor of being "biased" when race is mentioned at all (see Feagin et al. 1996; hooks 1994a; McIntosh 1998). This was most powerfully suggested in a fall first impression:

My first thought when I saw that he was black was that I would be hearing a lot about how much racism and prejudice he had faced on account of white people. . . . When I heard the teacher speak for a while I was no longer worried about this because he seemed to be intelligent and reasonable about it.

That bias, though, could also be perceived as some kind of a positive, as suggested by this spring first impression:

I am very ashamed of my next thoughts and wouldn't tell you them if I had to write my name, but the fact that you are African American caused me to have more interest in this class. This I know should not really play a role, and I am not sure why I feel the way I do.

My task, then, was to demonstrate that an explicit and complete awareness of the instructor's social positionings could be part of the overall learning experience, and used in empowering ways.

One of the many textual fragments I used in this effort was a mid-1990s advertisement for jeans from the Gap (see Figure 3.1), which I encountered in the *New York Times*. I introduced the ad during the second week of the fall semester (along with a place mat from McDonald's; see Figure 3.2), and the third week of the spring semester. The following field notes detail fall in-class reception of the Gap and McDonald's texts:

Shortly after soundscapes had class exercise: half of class talk about Gap ad, half talk about McDonald's place mat. Looks like we're starting off with low level of critical literacy, as most focused on aesthetics. (Anna's group talked about positions in Gap, OK given Anna's previous experience.) *Interesting thing:* seemed to be some uncomfortableness or, more accurately, 'Here we go'-ness when I

Figure 3.1. Gap Advertisment

Figure 3.2. McDonald's Place Mat

talked about racial implications. May have to address that overtly on Monday. Set it up nicely, I think: are multiple meanings, but have to say that there are multiple consequences. (Walt FN, September 10)

W. shows Gap and McDonald's ad. Students seem to be searching for meanings but so far, only covering surface. (Lori FN, September 10)

[Two students] laugh amongst themselves when walt asks class to look at expressions on the kid's faces. . . . i don't think the class liked it when walt was suggesting things about the expressions on the mcdonald's kids faces . . . i think they thought he was over-analyzing . . . that whole angry black male/why me? thing . . . don't think they expected to actually be ANALYZING commercials . . . probably thought they were just going to sit around and watch a bunch of cool clips or something. (Beeta FN, September 10)

Despite the better mood, I felt that today's discussion was as poor as Mon's. On Mon., the class seemed indifferent to the issues being raised, but today the class seemed to be . . . unprepared to discuss social issues concerning race. . . . Perhaps many of the students did not expect to be in a class that will discuss delicate social issues (especially the Frosh). I think a significant reason why Walt's 335 class ran so smoothly was because the majority of the students were prepared and deeply interested in tackling such social issues. My frosh. year, I took a media class with a similar name, but very different in nature to this course. (Rob FN, September 10)

While perhaps not as poorly prepared as Rob feels, the students were indeed surprised with the elements of sociological analysis of media and media texts. I expected this, not only because of general reluctance to discuss race with a minority instructor (even in my "race and ethnic relations" classes it took students a while to get comfortable talking about the issues), but because almost half of the students were in their very first semester of college and unsure of everything, especially in just their second week of the semester. They were also shy during the third week:

i really think the class is beginning to think that Walt has an agenda . . . like he's trying to cram race down their throats or something . . . i don't think they expected it to be such a central issue in the class . . . showing [an ad featuring the controversial rapper Ice Cube] probably added to some people's image of Walt as a bitter, angry black man . . . they just looked at him like "what the hell do you want from us?" (Beeta FN, September 15)

One interesting side note from W's discussion: When very directly asking class to guess why he might pay more attention to race than class, no one in room responds even after much probing. Why so reluctant to state obvious? Could some be afraid of insulting W? (Lori FN, September 15)

The students were, however, intrigued with some of the ads with strong racial elements and my encouragement to think sociologically about them. For example, students analyzed the following issues concerning the Gap ad (Figure 3.1): significance of gendered and racial layout (e.g., black man occupies lowest spot, and has the foot of a white woman on his shoulder), position of Asian woman in very center (interpreted by some as sign of "the model minority" [see Cho 1993; Kim 1993]), and ratio of whites to nonwhites (25 percent, interpreted by some as sign of progressive America since this roughly approximates current national ratio, and by others as inconsequential given positions of some minorities and exclusion of others, such as Latino/as). Similarly, for the McDonald's place mat (Figure 3.2), students debated the position and small size of the apparently angry African American children as opposed to the more prominent and more softly expressioned (whimsical, according to a few students) white child.

The Gap ad, further, was the most popular text for the first essay assignment, in which students were to pick a print advertisement from the class "image house" (a collection of texts on my Internet homepage) and discuss how their interpretation of the ad illustrated a sociological theory. While only one student chose the McDonald's place mat as his text, sixteen (of sixty-five) students choose the Gap ad (next most popular was a Mercedes-Benz spot featuring Marilyn Monroe, in eight essays). Their analyses, in general, were "safe," as they closely stuck to the essay guidelines and took neutral positions on reading the ad closely. That is, most students said that we should pay attention to the "meanings" of ads, but they didn't fully explore the implications of these meanings, and cautioned against going "too far," creating readings that aren't there. For instance, one student—contrary to my definition—insisted that "critique" is the project of finding negatives only, and this causes unnecessary tension between groups. Another student—Brenda—asked me (in the body of the essay) what I thought of the ad, and joked that I'd probably find something "weird" that no one else would. At least, though, they were becoming strongly aware that media texts are polysemic.

The spring class, on the other hand, was more willing to take up stronger positions. I also had the class provide sociological analysis of an advertisement as the first essay assignment, and the Gap ad was again the single most popular text, but the gap was not as large [nine of sixty-six texts, and the next most popular text—for Simple shoes (see Figure 3.3)—had six responses; the McDonald's place mat made four appearances] and the diversity of texts was greater (forty-two different texts versus thirty-two in the fall). This is due in part to the wider range of social experiences of those in the spring class. For instance, of the four usages of the McDonald's place mat, one student writes of matter-of-fact personal conviction and experience that racism is the fault of victims calling attention to it, the second references a similar assignment that her roommate completed for an upper-level telecommunications class, and the third said that she (regarding the model minority) "wouldn't have originally noticed anything controversial in the ad, however, our discussion in class has shown me otherwise." Further, two of the six Simple ad respondents mentioned previous personal memberships in the subculture of skateboarders (for which many Simple shoes are designed and marketed), discussing their appreciation of the referential self-denial of the ad, which is in line with the use of ironic individuality in their subculture (see Vanderbilt 1998:42–47).

The spring class was also much more active in the EC regarding the Gap ad and McDonald's place mats. Actually, I should say that they were active whereas the fall class was not, as fall students did not have any postings on these texts. This can be partly explained, though, by a

the product
is cool...

the Johnny™

so who gives a shit about the ad.

Pacific Sunwear   Journey's   Champs

U.S.A. & CANADA: 495 A South Fairview, Goleta CA 93117 (800) 611-0685
AUSTRALIA, NEW ZEALAND 61 (0) 44 41-5055 JAPAN 81 3 5421-3044 EUROPE 31 70 329 6134

Figure 3.3. Simple Advertisment

change made to the EC between semesters. In the fall the EC was entirely located on a system called "FirstClass," which is primarily a text-based system. Although it can display graphics files, it is cumbersome to do so, so I restricted postings to text, but (in the reflect house) said that students should talk about visits to various web sites, such as the image house on my web page. In the spring I added a system called "AltaVista," which is a web-based system: students use a web browser like Netscape to easily browse graphics and text. So while I retained course readings, the coffee house, and the debate house on FirstClass, I moved the reflect house to AltaVista, and added a discussion area in it for the image house.

I posted seven texts to the spring image house: the Gap ad, the McDonald's place mat, a Calvin and Hobbes cartoon, an Allen-Edmonds shoes ad, the Simple shoes ad, a Sega Saturn videogame system ad featuring Ice Cube, and the Mercedes-Benz ad featuring Marilyn Monroe. The Calvin and Hobbes text received the most posts (fifty-five), but this was because I required each student to respond to it in the first week of class to let me know that their AltaVista accounts were working. The other image house responses were completely voluntary, as students did not have to compose at least two messages for this house, as they did in the other three houses (as well as posting one message somewhere in the EC every week). The Gap ad received the most responses,[4] and students were not hesitant to engage one another:

In response to the Gap ad, I find the ad in a way humorous. Gap has gone out of its way to try to show the consumers that hey, every type of person wears our brand. However, I did find it kind of interesting how each person was set up, whether it be gender or race. It seems to be that in the ad all the women seem have these almost power positions. Most of the women are centered in the picture and have an arm or leg hanging on the guy nearest to them. On the other hand, looking at it from a race issue, it's interesting that both of the blacks in the picture are in corners of the ad, and the only oriental in the ad is in the center. However, I don't think Gap was doing any of this on purpose, but it is interesting to see that just through a simple ad such as this how gender and race issues could be found.

I agree that I don't think that there was a particular audience the producer was aiming for. If there was he or she might have only displayed that particular audience in the ad. Also since New York is a very diverse population, I feel that the ad was trying to get the message across that Gap jeans are for everyone and will fit everyone. I don't feel they were trying to do any narrowcasting or eliminate any person from their ad. This would be very unintelligent because it would discourage a certain group of people from buying their jeans, and then it would definitely not be a very effective ad.

This defense is just a little late, but some people seemed convinced that some of the subtexts in the Gap ad were accidental, particularly those involving the power relations between men and women. An opinion was expressed that the models may have just been posing naturally, stepping or sitting on the guys. I admit that in my photography "happy accidents" have occurred (something really cool but unintentional). However, the more people involved in the making of the photo the less likely that is. We are talking about a Gap ad with several professional models, their stylists, the company rep, probably two photo assistants and a photographer with a day rate of nearly $1,000. After it's shot the picture for the ad is picked by a highly paid and experienced art director. When something is done by a major advertiser for the *New York Times,* very little is left to chance. Anything that can be found in the photo was probably placed in the photo with very specific thought and intent. Just wanted to get that off my chest.

Welcome to multicultural America. The Gap ad gives you a fresh look at the many different ethnic races that make up this country. The ad almost seems too ideal in its representation of minorities. (Indeed, many changes have occurred since the 1960s.) I don't see the predominantly white readership of the *New York Times* being at all offended by such advertising, even though it does not cater to their interests. The minority in the country has had to battle its way up into receiving fair attribution in this country. It suffices to say that many factors played a role in elevating the minorities' status in the media. The greatest being the Civil Rights movement, and the Equal Opportunity Act. I viewed the ad as being a sign that minorities are finally receiving of fair attribution in the mass media. (This can easily be abused though. The so called 'United Colours' by Benetton, while attaining some artistic integrity, has been bashed for its treatment of white and black models in advertisements. These ads are in my mind racist, and vulgar. But, there's always someone who will call them art. Hey, they could be a good image to debate!)

As for the in-class operation of race in their reception of textual fragments like the Gap and McDonald's ads, the spring class, like the fall class, was a bit tight-lipped at first, especially when I explicitly referenced myself, in line with the teacher as text project. For instance, to illustrate the concept of hegemony I asked the students to consider their first impressions of who they would regard as more informative and useful in two cases: (a) I'm the instructor, [white male student] was graduate assistant, and (b) we were both anonymous grad students at a conference. The students eagerly discussed case (a), stating that they would view me as the authority, but were reluctant on case (b): "No one wanted to speak up about the race issue in the you and [student] experiment. Either the class is very polite or it was something they hadn't thought of" (Jennifer FN, January 28). Indeed, the issue and concept were new to most, but an additional reason was that they were reluctant to enter the matrix of domination and consider their own racial privileges, especially that early in the semester. As we'll see in later chapters, however, the students became more outspoken later in each semester as they gained experience and comfort with my pedagogical techniques.

I will conclude this chapter with a brief look at dynamics of one additional day in each semester of the autoethnography. Whereas most days and topics concerned visual media, "the consumption of music" was about an aural medium. I chose to include this topic to not only further explore the multiple dimensions of electronic media, but to provide a nice change of pace. The students appreciated this move.

Phil—intervention "failed"

Accepting [media] as a shallow way to blow a few bucks protects you from the ill-effects that are constantly blamed on television. People like me don't become desensitized to violence, they become desensitized to Hollywood violence. The real world is on this side of the screen. —PHIL, CONCLUSION TO FINAL PROJECT (on the movie *Tin Cup*)

Like Nate, Phil—a junior from the spring class—takes pride in possessing a strong sense of cynicism about the media. Unlike Nate, Phil never connected the worthy project of media wariness with the possibility of using it toward socially empowering ends. From start to finish Phil viewed the media as a distraction (though a necessary one) in contemporary American society:

First off, I hate watching sports. There's just something sad about sitting on the couch and watching other people exercise. I did happen to catch the second half of the superbowl because I left my house, and I'm pretty sure anywhere I would have went I would have seen it. The second half's commercials were a disappointment. I don't know what the standard air time to sales formula is, maybe even a lousy commercial on gameday brings an exponential sales increase, but I hope not. I didn't see anything that swayed me, but I'm sure others did. And when did nike stop trying to sell ability in a shoe (buy this shoe and play like…) and start trying to sell drive (buy this shoe and you actually might jog, or at least "You can …") Why can't they just show me a shoe? Nike's had one good commercial in the last five years, and It was charles barkley saying "If you buy my shoe, you'll own nice shoes. That's all." (response to debate house question on favorite Super Bowl ads)

Note that in this posting Phil implicitly criticizes Nike's excessive commodification of athletic gear. From the beginning of class Phil demonstrated an understanding of the political economy of media culture. For instance, in the second week of class students were asked to visit Sony's web site as the starting point for reflect house discussion. Phil writes that

With a search engine on the opening page, I'd say they are at least taking steps to simplify. One of the biggest drawbacks of the internet is its speed. Consumers aren't used to waiting for a page to load, or anything else for that matter, so web designers have had to come up with ways of speeding things along without sacrificing content. I doubt you can find exactly what you're looking for without distractions, but what you buy is your choice. Also, understand this is Sony.com, one of the broadest headings imaginable. I can only guess as to how large this group of sites is, but I would be willing to bet the same amount of information in print would be nearly unmanageable.

Phil's critical literacy skills were not altered by the *I Like It Like That* readings. On the first reading (his first time seeing the movie) he writes that the clip was "fairly entertaining, decent Sunday afternoon fare (Is it fare or fair?)" and "characters are tired and overused. Short tempered Latino woman, materialistic egotistical white guy." On the second reading he writes "how many times have I seen this plot and changed the channels? Plenty," and that the "stereotypes of Rigid Whites and casual Latin Americans are amusing." He concludes that his critical reactions have changed "little."

One reason why the attempt to create a stronger sociological imagination seemed to fail with Phil was that many of the texts I used in class did not hold personal interest for him, as indicated by the above EC posting about the Super Bowl, and these two posts:

This site seemed pretty worthless to me, but as stated by another "I've never been a 14 year old girl." I would assume if they say their target is 14 year olds, it's probably a little younger, I'm pretty sure that's how teen publications work. (All the 15 year olds read *Seventeen* and so on). It seemed so mixed, shallow sexual advice and feminism recruiting. I don't feel I took anything away with me. (week 4 reflect house, about the feminist webzine gURL)

Anyone else out there ever try to use web radio? For the uninitiated, web radio is just like broadcast, only over the internet and therefore without the restriction of distance. From random club music out of London to a blues channel in Mississippi, radio now has the potential for nearly limitless audiences. I'm very excited about the idea (since, for the most part Bloomington radio seems to suck), but I still am unable to get it to work properly. I guess my modem is a little too slow. (week 6 coffee house)

As indicated, Phil did not get anything out of gURL, which is a web site created for thirteen to seventeen-year-old girls, and I never talked about web radio in class. Perhaps the inclusion of texts and issues that Phil was passionate about would have helped shift his thinking about electronic media culture. Probably not, as Phil identifies himself as a "slacker," which he says are those who resist the speedup of American life and—as a matter of principle—participate as little as possible in traditional media and consumer cultures. Phil was the only student in either class to create his media journal on his World Wide Web page. When I asked him (via e-mail) about the apparent contradiction in doing extra work for the assignment, he responded (also via e-mail) that it wasn't extra work, since compiling examples and appending discussion would be easier for him than searching other media, as he was on-line a lot. I should also note that his response came *after* grades were submitted; he said that he didn't want his answer to alter my opinion of him and affect his grade.

Interestingly, Phil participated in *The X-Files* salon project of chapter 6. I believe, though, that he did it mostly for the credit and an easy "A" (he also earned an "A" in s101). In a sense, Phil did use the media in a personally empowering way: to help himself graduate from college. So, while Phil's reaction to the spring s101 class represents a failure in my specific attempt to enable students to use media culture as a positive force for social change, it can be viewed as an instance when a student appropriated elements for personal advancement. The division between "failed" and "successful" intervention, it seems, is more of a Möbius strip than a sharp line in cement. Indeed, that is what makes postmodern spaces like Pensieves so interesting.

The Consumption of "The Consumption of Music"

W. asks if anyone thinks rap isn't music. No one says a word. He says, "Come on, I won't hurt you." Interesting comment. Questions: (1) Could this have been an attempt to make class feel "safe" about critiquing rap, a genre stereotypically defined as the only music Afr.-Amer's listen to and create/perform? If so, what are implications? (2) Could this be example of no-win situation faced by Afr-Amers? That is, by distancing himself from rap, W. could be charged with elitism, etc., yet by associating himself with rap, reinforces stereotype that ALL black men listen to rap and that rap is the ONLY music all black people listen to. (3) Could it also have worked in similar ways in relation to stereotype that all black men are angry, violent, hostile, etc? (Lori FN, October 22)

On a Wednesday in the fall of the autoethnography I centered the day's topic of "the consumption of music" on "sampling," the practice of incorporating portions of other songs (lyrics and or/music) into new songs. This art form is most often associated with rap; in fact some call it one of rap's defining characteristics (Rose 1994). Sampling is used in other genres, however, though many students were surprised by this. In anticipation of that reaction, I had assembled a montage of musical selections. In addition to a rap selection (tracks from the Fugees' "The Score" album), I played a track from an avant-garde classical music group (the Kronos Quartet) sampling a rock standard (Jimi Hendrix's "Purple Haze"), another classical collaboration (vocalist Bobby McFerrin and cellist Yo-Yo Ma) sampling the same thing, a fusion of jazz and hip-hop (by the group Buckshot LeFonque), and an alternative rock group sampling spoken verse (the group Portishead).

Lori's field note got at social issues involving perceptions of sampling. In addition to race and class (the students initially thought it the province of working- and "under" class African American and Latino youth), Lori brought up issues of gender, both to the class as a whole and to students sitting around her:

Nate [of the first student spotlight box] says (just to me and another student) that rap is more explicitly degrading of women. I'm surprised to hear him say this, so I very simply ask him if he recalls that "classic" metal hit, in which AC/DC tells us we'd better "lock up our daughters" because he's "TNT, DY-NOMITE!!!" I'm ready to ramble on, but he gets my point.

Throughout class Lori either elaborated on points that I or other students had made [such as on historical conditions surrounding the African American communication pattern of call-and-response, which is the basis of much of rap (see Rose 1994)], or anticipated directions in which I was moving. Throughout the semester the 494 crew would raise pertinent questions and/or comments, though Lori was the most consistent in this process. This was expected, as she was the assistant with the most experience with sociology in general and me and my interests in particular (she was, recall, my very first teaching assistant).

Lori was also responsible for posting questions to the fall debate house in the EC, where students discussed a single specific question set for each week, as opposed to the open-ended coffee house where students talked about whatever they wanted, or the reflect house, where the focus was narrow (a single web site), but the approach was broad (could pose questions, provide analysis, allude to other texts, etc.). In week 7 (covering the consumption of music), though, I posted the question, which basically asked the students to discuss whether or not sampling was "theft, or creative," in line with a student's interpretation of one of the readings for the week:

After reading Strauss's article I totally agree with what he is saying. I think that you are not a true musician if you are taking samples from other songs and using them for yourself. I believe that you are stealing when you use other peoples' songs. And how can you think that you will ever be successful in the music world if you can't even write your own songs? You need to develop your own style then later on down the road after you are already a success I don't feel like it would be such a big deal if you "sampled" somebody else's song. (coffee house posting, moved to start week 7 debate house)

Of the fifteen responses to my reposting of this message as the week 7 debate house questions, twelve were in agreement, and generally panned sampling as uncreative and theft. The three counterarguments were made by Jennifer, Anna, and "Nate." This is one of the cases, it seems, when the attempt to actualize the sociological imagination failed, as students ignored larger historical and social contextualization provided by Lori and me. Aside from the quip that "I won't hurt you" when discussing rap as music, I did not share any of my personal experiences and thoughts, but let the discussion in class and in the EC flow unchanneled. While, of course, you can never predict exact articulations in the classroom as Pensieve, this does suggest that fully implementing the teacher as text strategy is needed throughout, especially when the class does not have a lot of lived experiences of its own to draw on. Of course, students can—and did—draw on other types of practices (such as abstract concepts and empirical studies) to increase critical literacy (and, indeed, these are powerful and useful tools), but the teacher as text calls for the use of lived experience in creating the sociological imagination—hence this particular teacher as text intervention did not work.

The spring class had a more eclectic reaction to the texts under investigation: "The sampling discussion begins. There are many diverse opinions about this. Some think sampling is okay, some think it is okay at times, and others don't like it because it steals from great old songs" (Jennifer FN, March 2). We went on to put those opinions into sociological perspective, focusing on how our socioeconomic class positions influence taste and standards. One thing that we did not do was explicitly look at race:

Why is it okay for certain artists to sample and not for others? Why can Portishead sample and have it be okay but Puffy is considered a thief? Of course much of this depends on taste but still, I am quite curious about any sort of racist connotation mixed in with this. Imagine if we would have had any African-American students in class. Would they have felt isolated by the predominantly white middle-class classroom and their opinions on sampling, especially with their condemnation of a black artist? The students can flesh this out (at least some of them) in the Debate House. (Jennifer FN, March 2)

Unfortunately, it was not fleshed out in the debate house, primarily because it was not explicitly referenced in Jennifer's instructions for the week. As we'll see in the next chapter, race is not a topic the students will explore if they don't have to. Why did I not bring up this specific issue, either in class when students were mostly anti-Puff Daddy (who was, at the time, a highly visible black hip-hop artist who uses sampling in every song) or in the EC? I didn't do it in the debate house as I generally held a hands-off policy there, only posting comments when Lori or Jennifer could not, or when a student made a comment that misrepresented a theory or issue presented in class. I did not explicitly discuss the racial components in class in order to reduce the perception that race was an obsession and that I was "biased." In line with observations like those made by Lori and Beeta in the field notes cited earlier in the chapter, sometimes I could not fully explore racial implications or I would risk turning off the class. The teacher as text is, indeed, quite the high-wire act.

I also let the racial elements remain submerged because Puff Daddy had his defenders in class, as well as his detractors. Also, soon after showing a video of one of Puff's then-current hits ("Been Around the World") I discussed the call-and-response musical tradition, and stated that our tastes operate out of cultural socialization. So, while I did not explicitly state that race plays a role in cultural socialization, some may have made that connection.

An articulation that *was* made in the spring debate house that was absent in the fall was that the sociological imagination is involved in music appreciation, as expressed in these two postings:

Of course we all have our own take on this issue—we are all different people with different "sociological imaginations"—thus whether i think a cover, sample, or a remake is good or bad is obviously relative. I have to agree with what [student] is saying about original artists—ones who compose their own music, sing, and play the instruments. I am very partial to female artists probably because i am female—However there are many male artists/groups whom i also appreciate.

Whether covers, samplings or remixes are creative or not can never be concretely determined because everyone has different opinions and good arguments to back their opinions up, as can be seen by reading everyone's entries. . . . As a dancer and choreographer who loves performing I know that I use other people's steps they have made up in some of my dances and it's not because I am not trying to be original, but rather I liked a certain move and wanted to use it again. I suppose this could be related to sampling because I connect the steps with ones of my own, but it is possible that some other choreographer used the same step, both of us thinking it was original, but it isn't. There are only so many notes in the world and ways to arrange them, and if someone makes a song that is enjoyable and happen to use something from another artist I think that is great.

In general, the twenty-eight responses to Jennifer's topic expressed a nuanced approach, trying to look at both good and bad elements of sampling. On balance, they were generally positive, as opposed to the overwhelmingly negative reaction in the fall. Again, this is the result of the higher level of direct experience members of the spring had with issues related to the texts: there were several students in the spring class who were very familiar with art worlds and their practices (such as the choreographer, and the photographer in the third Gap image house citation), who voiced perspectives that engaged others. Two of the twenty-eight responses, for instance, were from students who usually did not post anything in the EC.

Overall, in both fall and spring semesters students were very interested in the sampling controversy and other issues concerning the consumption of music, as summed up by the opening to a spring debate house posting: "WOW! Such debate over music!" The classroom as Pensieve is a place where students and teachers both question the knowledge that is produced in that site. Instructors explicitly call attention to the ways in which forces such as disciplinary alignment, racial and ethnic discourses, local social movements, and national political-economic conditions constrain some knowledges and facilitate others. Students, in turn, are encouraged to struggle with these articulations in many ways, while also challenging instructors to back up their claims. Although they did not always utilize their sociological imaginations to the fullest extent to connect experiences, textual fragments, and contexts, the students were engaged by topics such as the consumption of music, and enthusiastically debated them. That is, indeed, a very important and necessary condition for creating the college classroom as Pensieve.

Chapter Four

Strange Texts in Postmodern Space

It is possible for students simultaneously to be very canny about the social forces that define their identity and still take their own subject position as the real itself, against which radical differences are dismissed as bizarre. Even though the day-to-day experiences of contemporary students includes complex negotiations with difference across lines of gender, race, class, religion, etc., these differences are often softened by an off-hand, hip, MTVeejay style that can be adopted by almost anyone young. Encounters with truly strange texts and experiences are rare.

— THOMAS MCLAUGHLIN, *Street Smarts and Critical Literacy*

The "teacher as text" project involves exposing students to new texts and experiences, exploding the texts into sociological components of analysis like race, class, age, and gender, and explicating new narratives that help students comprehend just how complicated their social worlds are, that differences that they perceive as radical and bizarre may not be as easily dismissed as they'd desire. In my classes I expose students to "strange texts" (Jacobs and Brooks 1999), media products that most have not encountered, and which preclude the easy assimilation described by McLaughlin. Such texts are intertextual: decoding of meanings are dependent on knowledge and use of other media products and messages and resulting lived experiences, even if the products have apparently clear and discreet boundaries. Encounters with strange texts force students to speak the lower frequencies, raising usually background understandings of social structural connections to the conscious level in order to explicitly deal with implications of their particular articulations.

This is most vividly illustrated by using the short HBO film *Space Traders* (Hudlin and Hudlin 1994), about extraterrestrial aliens visiting earth with an extraordinary social engineering proposal. I show this film to almost all my classes; in this chapter I will explore individual class reception of the text when used in the 1997–1998 autoethnography. I will also explore another "strange text," an episode of the TV show *The X-Files*. In the classroom as Pensieve one of the tasks of the instructor is to expose students to unusual texts such as these, helping students learn that forces exist in their lives that are more complex than they'd care to admit. Although the texts may already be part of the students' lives in one way or another, in the Pensieve the way in which students relate to the text can be made strange, highlighting the unusual—but very powerful—considerations that students have not investigated.

What Is Space Traders?

There was no escape, no alternative. Heads bowed, arms now linked by slender chains, black people left the New World as their forebears had arrived.
            —DERRICK BELL, "The Space Traders"

"The Space Traders" is a short story by Derrick Bell in his *Faces at the Bottom of the Well* (1992), and *Space Traders* is an HBO film adaptation (Hudlin and Hudlin 1994) of that story. I showed the forty-minute film to both classes of the 1997–1998 autoethnography, during the ninth (fall) and fourth (spring) weeks of the semester. Then, in a five-page essay assignment students were asked to choose and analyze an important difference in the two treatments, and to discuss implications of their articulations.

Both versions depict the United States in the year 2000. The nation is burdened economically with a deficit, faces energy problems, suffers from severe environmental hazards, and continues to struggle with the issue of race. However, all these social ills can be solved if the country surrenders its African American citizens to a group of extraterrestrial travelers—"space traders"—who will turn the Statue of Liberty into gold, clean up polluted waterways, and provide the country with a source of unlimited energy in exchange. The American government is given a set time period (five days in the film, seventeen in the story) to decide whether to accept the offer. What happens on judgment day is far less important, however, than what is revealed over the course of the time period about the country and Americans of all persuasions. As the American government leaves the final decision to its citizens through a national telephone referendum, the story explores responses to the trade offer from the country's government, its commercial culture industries, and its citizens, particularly its African Americans. As black people mount traditional strategies of resistance—sit-ins, rallies, and boycotts—American captains of industry wage a massive campaign (largely through the media) to shape the consciousness of Americans. Despite these efforts, the majority of the citizens vote to surrender blacks to the space traders.[1]

This section's epigraph is taken from the closing sentences of the short story. Bell (1992) constructs the story in a way that strongly suggests that blacks were, are, and will be sacrificed when such sacrifices serve the nation's interests. In other essays in *Faces at the Bottom of the Well*, he argues that these sacrifices are based on a racism that is a permanent component of American life, and emphasizes the urgency to move beyond the belief that time and the altruism of Americans will solve the country's racial problems (see also hooks 1995). The video adaptation, however, does not make such a strong articulation. For instance, while at the end of the film African Americans are also beamed aboard the traders' ships, this is not done in chains, and, further, they are allowed one piece of carry-on luggage, suggesting that they are guests going to a better place. Indeed, it is such rich textual polysemy that makes the film version an excellent text for debate in the project of constructing the classroom as Pensieve.

Space Traders in the Fall

Eliza says "Why are they still making a big deal since they got them off campus . . . isn't that why they had the rally?" (Lori FN, October 29)

[Eliza] doesn't understand what minorities are still complaining about. "ABC got expelled off the campus, isn't that what they wanted?" Prior to this comment, she interrupted another student with support of ABC. (Rob FN, October 29)

Two weeks before I screened *Space Traders* in the fall, the campus newspaper broke a story that the pledge class of one of the fraternities, ABC, had been arrested while attempting to steal a street sign, and that a list of other assigned tasks on a scavenger hunt was confiscated.[2] Controversy soon flared over the racist, sexist, and classist nature of the list, such as instructions to take pictures with (among other things) "funny-looking Mexicans," and both "ugly" and "hot" women. Predictably, the house claimed that it was not racist or sexist, and that the list was created by a few rogues and was not officially sanctioned. After rallies and marches by a coalition of several minority groups, and a hearing before various judiciary bodies, the fraternity was expelled. Eliza was reacting to possible further action by the coalition, such as an effort to establish a set long-term time limit before the fraternity could reapply for campus membership.

In the week before *Space Traders,* one entire class period was devoted to the controversy (centered around media representations), and a lively debate flourished in the EC. As could be expected, students who were members of sororities and fraternities tended to resist institutional analyses of the Greek system (preferring individual "bad apple" accounts, and that the controversy was "blown out of proportion"), but there was considerable diversity in the fifty-three postings. Twenty-nine of these were in the coffee house, and the remainder (twenty-four) were in the debate house, centering on whether the campus newspaper (*Indiana Daily Student, IDS* for short) should publish the scavenger hunt list:

- The list needs to be printed and not edited. It is our right to see for ourselves what the list consisted of. As students we need to be informed of what is happening on our campus and that is one example. It was hard for me to believe that someone would actually compose something as stupid, racist, and sexist as this.
- Before the *IDS* prints the scavenger hunt list, I think they need to contemplate the reason for printing it. Is it to raise awareness or is it to circulate newspapers?
- I do believe that ABC should be severely punished, maybe even kicked off of campus. An example needs to be made and this is the opportunity to do so. While I will not pretend that some hazing does exist in other houses, I stress that it is important not to generalize and assume that everyone in the greek system is a part of it or experiences it.
- I truly believe the *IDS* is an example of the negative effects of media. The incident has been blown out of proportion.
- Well we still have freedom of the press in this country, so the *IDS* had the right to publish the scavenger hunt list.
- Just a note to the women who are in sororities: If you are standing by the ABCs and supporting them, I want you to stop and think a moment about the content of the list, not as members of a sorority, but exclusively as women. How does it make you feel when an organization of men is demeaning you?

The point for our purposes here is twofold: (1) the debate indicated that students had, indeed, begun to think more critically about their social worlds in general, and (2) many students entered *Space Traders* week with heightened sensitivity to the effects of stratification and inequality on a personal level.

Eliza (subject of this section's epigraph) epitomizes this. She is a member of a sorority (one that worked closely with the expelled fraternity) and initially resisted entry into the matrix of domination, as Lori notes:

At times like this, I don't envy Walt's job. No, Missy, that's not the only reason they (those troublesome blacks and other undesirables) had the rally . . . it was *one* of reasons they had the rally. They also had it so that people like you, in your smug, privileged bubbles, will be forced to take a peek at the real world outside. And the point Walt brought up has nothing to do with whether or not ABCs are off campus. He's talking about the fact that minority groups were excluded from the decision making process altogether . . . two separate issues. (Lori FN, October 29)

Eliza later expanded her perspectives after being forced to grapple with *Space Traders*. At the end of her essay on *Space Traders* she wrote: "In conclusion, I really enjoyed this part of our class. I thought it was a very unique kind of paper that made you really think about how people in today's society can be." As will be discussed, other students came to similar conclusions. This was not, however, an easy process:

Very briefly discussed color-blindness and valuing diversity as broad approaches to race relations. Man, I miss s335 and more sophisticated discussion. (Walt FN, October 29)

This class makes me nauseous with their apathy. (Beeta FN, October 29)

Walt getting frustrated that nobody is responding to his questions . . . most of them legitimate and well-posed. I'm getting annoyed too. (Lori FN, October 29)

Ultimately, I think today's poor discussion had little to do with Walt and a lot to do with "generation-I-don't-give-a-fuck." (Rob FN, October 29)

As can be deduced from these selections from our field notes, overall we became frustrated during the discussion about *Space Traders*. Recall, however, that each of us had been in at least one other sociology s335 "race and ethnic relations" class in which the text was very enthusiastically and intricately debated. S335 classes were taken mainly by juniors and seniors, as opposed to the majority freshman and sophomore fall s101 class. Note, also, that s335 is an elective mainly satisfying sociology major requirements, whereas s100-level classes serve many other purposes, such as a campus-wide requirement to take a "cultural studies" class. Part of our disappointment was the result of an unfair comparison with a class that was older and more motivated by the subject matter in and of itself.

It was my job to turn that frustration into something more positive. I had to find ways to get students motivated by the text and the over-arching project of becoming critical social agents. Keeping the lesson learned in the previous week's fraternity scavenger hunt in mind—students enthusiastically respond and ponder issues when they sense that personal interests are at stake—I tried a "radical" idea after twenty minutes of relatively bland discussion:

Whoa!!! Walt gets bold . . . he asks us to anonymously vote on trade. (Lori FN, October 29)

Wow! I never thought he would do something so radical . . . I mean, that's pretty radical for Walt. (Beeta FN, October 29)

The class thought so too, as there were numerous gasps of surprise and shocked expressions when I asked the class to simulate the vote taken in the film and anonymously disclose whether they would vote yes or no to this question: "If the space traders asked for all African Americans today, how would *you* vote?" Each student wrote "yes" or "no" on a slip of paper, folded it so that neighbors could not discern their vote, and passed the slips to the front of the room, where I collected them.

The students were also astonished when I announced that "most of these are yes votes" as I counted the ballots, and breathed a collective sigh of relief when I said "just kidding" ten seconds later. Then, just before I got to the end I said "This one says 'yes, and I would start with you first, Walt.'" This time they knew I was joking right off, and laughed immediately. Later, however, Lori told me that she had dared Nate (who is, recall, one of the two spotlighted students in chapter 3) to write that down, and that when I "read" it she told him she was only joking, to which he insisted he didn't write it. The upshot was that Nate did become more vocal (and more critical) in the ensuing debate (perhaps to prove that he wasn't "racist"?). Alexander (1999:309) wonders, "how does [students'] construction of Black masculine identity 'derail' my own construction and collide with my instructional role as teacher?" My "radical" move is an intentional way of demonstrating how "the auto-ethnographic text emerges from the researcher's bodily standpoint as [he] is continually recognizing and interpreting the residue traces of culture inscribed upon [his] hide from interacting with others in contexts" (Spry 2001:711): I make an often abstract issue (race) real and live for students in the classroom by including myself in the process.

Why was it termed "radical"? Operating in "the teacher as text" project, I usually present numerous fragments of media messages and products, and make temporary articulations in the effort to try to get students to make their own multisided articulations. In other words, I force students into the gray in order to negotiate the increasing grays of our lives. The mock vote, however, forced them into a black/white situation. Rob, though, prefers this. Here he comments on my repeated efforts to get the two students who actually wrote "yes" to identify themselves:

There were some things I would have done differently, and on a few occasions I was frustrated with Walt's methods and strategies. That's very easy for me to say as an objective observer from the outside however. . . . Nonetheless, I would not have asked the 2 yes people to identify themselves so many times. I understand that had one of those people stepped forward, the discussion would have exponentially increased in vitality, but the cost of appearing desperate was too great.

This note illustrates three interesting issues concerning the autoethnographic process. First, the methodological issue of "objectivity" raises its head. Rob goes on to describe how his note-taking suffered a bit as he became frustrated with the class's (lack of) responses. Autoethnographies, recall, are not concerned with capturing a complete process, but fragments that create heuristics. Researchers, further, are interested in charting the operation of power, of which "objectivity" claims are of prime interest, often effacing inequality (Gieryn 1994; Haraway 1990, 1991). In this effort, capturing the researchers' own reactions *as affected by the space under study* are extremely valuable. Participation in postmodern spaces involves hyperreflexivity; a study of the classroom as Pensieve demands that instructors/researchers and their practices be as much an empirical object/subject as the students.

Rob's frustrations were useful theoretically, as I drew upon them to develop my articulation of autoethnography (explored in chapter 2). Investigating the autoethnographers' frustrations can have tangible empirical effects as well. During the discussion of the ABC affair, Beeta made an in-class comment that it was not surprising that ABC got caught, as "fraternity boys have the collective IQ of soup." Later in the week she posted a note in the EC saying that the statement was meant to provoke: "That is why we are all here, in this class, to learn to think critically, to challenge the ways in which we normally perceive the world, above all, to *think*." She admitted, though, that part of the comment was spurred by frustration with the then low level of engagement with larger issues. In the same spirit as Amy Lee (2000:20), Beeta used her authority to "advocate [for alternative knowledges], to acknowledge them and articulate why they were valuable, but we could only enact them together." The students used her "outburst" and explanation of its rationale to rethink their own agency, as noted in these EC responses following the class:

- In the beginning I thought people were blowing the whole ABC thing out of proportion, until I heard the list in class on Monday. I was surprised and shocked about some of the things that were said in it. . . . And Beeta, I am glad to hear that your statement was only to stir up the class. It really pissed me off when I heard it.
- Kudos to you Beeta for attempting to stir the class up!
- In regard to the ABC issues, I personally think that ABC should get their charter pulled. I plan on attending the rally this evening to show my support.

In that class as well as during *Space Traders* week, however, many others remained silent or voiced neutral, safe thoughts. Turning to the second of the three autoethnography issues, Kamala Visweswaran (1994) reminds us that silences can be just as empirically and theoretically informative as audible discourse. Theoretically, it supports Collins's (1991) arguments that we resist full entry into the matrix of domination: the white class was reluctant to examine aspects of white privilege with their African American instructor. Empirically, we observe that the silences were strategic, as the class became more vocal in the more impersonal medium of the electronic classroom and more private medium of the essay:

The fact that the story was written by African-Americans may say something about the way whites and blacks want to deal with racial issues. This is exclusively my opinion, but I believe that white people think that there is little racism left in the world and would like to ignore the racism that there is. On the other hand, I believe that because racism affects blacks more than whites, black people don't want the issue ignored. (EC response)

As an audience member the comparison allowed me to feel the intense pressure and frustration felt by the blacks. I was able to connect with the minority group, as I am sure others did as well. (Essay response)

This story was a great wake up call. (Essay response)

I think a problem with widely broadcasting a text like this as a learning tool rather than a source of entertainment is that it could create a lot of paranoia and heightened tension and resentment between whites and blacks. (EC response)

I would have to disagree with [3 students]. Shows like *Space Traders* cause a lot of uproar, a lot of uproar we don't need. (EC response)

I never asked my black acquaintances [about group treatment in America] because that doesn't make for polite conversation. (Essay response)

Little did I know that I would experience one of the worst realizations of my life. (Essay response)

Overall, thirty-seven students posted messages concerning *Space Traders* in the EC (twenty-seven in the debate house, ten in the coffee house), and all completed the second essay. These responses indicate that, one way or the other, most students did engage the issues, in a variety of ways and from a variety of perspectives. Again, it is not the job of instructors to police politically correct thought in the classroom as Pensieve, but to help students investigate the ways "in which discourse, imagine, and desire intersect with the operations of material relations of power to foreground the ways in which power is deployed, experienced, and made productive within and across multiple spheres of daily life" (Giroux 2000:7). Note, also, that teachers should deconstruct their positions as well as students, as "excitement is generated through collective effort" (hooks 1994a:8), especially when we realize that "we may learn and grow in circumstances where we do not feel safe, that the presence of conflict is not necessarily negative but rather its meaning is determined by how we cope with that conflict" (hooks 2003:64).

Third, Rob's field note points to the difficulty of striking a balance between asking too much and too little of students with regard to critical social agency. When students' taken-for-granted understandings are displaced, and when they are confronted with multiple articulations about societal haves and have-nots, students often become angry, blaming the teacher for making them "think" (hooks 1994a; McLaughlin 1996). Some wrestle with the challenge constructively, but some yearn for simpler days in which they were comfortably oblivious to the operation of power at the level of the everyday, and resist systematic analysis. Teachers must reveal their own frustrations and ambivalences to help students sort through theirs. This is what I did at the end of Wednesday's class:

Walt says something about "would vote not pass, or would everybody just say fuck the niggas???" Whoa . . . Never heard him react so passionately. Maybe that's needed today. (Lori FN, October 29)

Walt says "fuck 'em." I bet he really wants to say this to the class. (Rob FN, October 29)

Nate asks me if Walt just said "fuck" but skips the "nigga" part. I say "fuck yea he did." (Lori FN, October 29)

I went on to say that I would not clearly articulate my personal thoughts on the trade, but asked the students to think about the implications of the statement, given who was saying it. Spry (2001:706) notes, "in performed autoethnography, the research artist is the existential nexus upon which the research rotates, deviates, and gyrates presenting through performance critical self-reflexive analysis of [his] own experiences of dissonance and discovery with others." I wanted to use this aspect of autoethnography to active the Pensieve's function as a space in which the participants actively and reflexively ponder the effects of the spatial environment on meaning creation and dissemination, combining fragments to form situated, partial, and heuristic understandings.

That, indeed, was the case. In the last ten minutes of class I asked the class what they would think if I told them I thought the trade would pass if proposed that year (1997). Forty percent thought I was just being a devil's advocate, and 60 percent believed I was serious. Several people raised their hands to comment, including one who had not spoken to that point, and the class left in a buzz. Lori and Rob, however, disagree on the efficacy of this move:

I also question Walt's decision to ask the class if they would be surprised to learn that he thinks the trade would pass today. Why even let them entertain the notion that you think it may not pass. I for one think it would pass today, hands down, and I'm confident that Walt feels the same, so why offer these privileged, apathetic whiteys the luxury of dismissing this whole argument on the grounds that even their pro-black, African-American instructor doesn't think it would pass? I say take a stance and defend it with supportive arguments. I'm sure Walt has some theoretical reason involving teacher–student objectivity to explain his motive. (Rob FN, October 29)

I think he is playing advocate to some extent, as is reflected in the fact that he even had to ask if class took him seriously. If he was confident enough in his own statement, why take vote to see if class believed him or not. Also, just based on previous comments I've heard from Walt—both in class and outside of class—I really am a little surprised to hear him commit himself so determinedly one way or the other. We've spent so much time talking about *Space Traders* and related issues, and at times I've been confused about W's personal beliefs. There have been times when I've thought his politics/views were really radical, Afro-centric even, and there have been other occasions when I wasn't quite so sure. I don't think I've ever thought of him as being conservative, but moderate about some issues perhaps. I guess the point is, because we've spent soooo much time talking about such issues, I really wasn't able to so easily decide one way or the other whether or not he was being serious. Paradoxical, I guess, but in a way it makes sense that since I've probably seen more sides of Walt than others in class, I would have more difficult time. And the same can be said about me: since he knows me better than others in class, he'd probably have to do a lot more weighing when trying to figure out my views on particular subjects. Whatever the case, I think this was W's best *Space Traders* lecture yet. (Lori FN, October 29)

Rob is right—I did have a theoretical justification in mind, and that was to make sure I was practicing political education instead of politicizing education (Giroux 1996). I wanted to call attention to the operation of power/knowledge (Foucault 1980, 1978) and its consequences, rather than building a rigid, doctrinaire hierarchy of power that effaces very pertinent traces of its construction. Lori's note gets at that point. Articulations slide, collide, and mutate; I wanted the students to begin to think about what particular elements of their experiences they will foreground, and which they will push into the background, based on the dynamics of particular contexts in which those articulations are made.

The use of language is an important consideration in that effort. For instance, some students may object to the use of expletives for any number of reasons, and others may be offended by the use of terms that have historically been used to degrade and police certain social groups. Indeed, the use of terms like "fuck" and "nigger" can be extremely volatile, and reinforce systems of domination if left unmarked. On the other hand, we can use such language to encourage our students and ourselves to investigate how language works in circuits of power and how it may be redeployed to serve alternative interests. It may take time to develop sufficient rapport in order to conduct this project (see Jacobs 1998), but it is an integral component in the attempt to create the classroom as Pensieve. The 494 crew and I did not receive any complaints about the use of potentially disturbing language. On the contrary, this seemed to enhance classroom experiences for some students, as suggested by this comment on a fall course evaluation:

[Walt is] the type of guy you'd want as a friend. Sometimes he swears or uses expressions like college kids do. That is what helps people learn and makes it fun.

So, through a combination of exposure to the strange text of *Space Traders,* and creating connections (for both students and instructors) between it, other texts, larger social issues, and personal experiences, and signaling that it is OK—and, in fact, encouraged!—to take risks and articulate potentially unpopular ideas and beliefs, I advanced the project of creating the classroom as Pensieve. After the student spotlight box I turn to analysis of use of the text during the spring semester.

Kate—intervention "failed"

[Kate] has not learned much. Too little support for contention that going to multiracial high school automatically makes one critical.—WALT FN, November 22 (regarding essay 2)

In any class teachers are likely to find students who will try to figure out exactly what the teacher wants from them and then not deviate from that path (even if deviation is the name of the game, as in my classes). Kate—a freshman from the fall—is such a student. She brought me rough drafts of each essay and the final project before they were due, and tried to give me what she thought I wanted to hear. As suggested by the above comment, she was content to grasp the general outline of social processes, never taking my encouragement to dig into the nuances and question received wisdom.

Consider Kate's posting on *Space Traders* (week 10 debate house):

I agree with [two students]. While programs like Space Traders can be educational in that they open people's eyes, I can also see viewers talking of it as a joke since in real life that can never happen. It definitely opened up my eyes, however we watched it for class and I knew we would have to write on it. If this program was on as I was flipping through the channels at home, I would not watch it because it is so blown out of proportion. When watching TV, most people don't want to be reminded of problems in society, they take shows for what they are, entertainment and ignore the actual meaning producers had in mind.

Note that Kate says that she read *Space Traders* critically only because she had to, and would not normally do this. Kate, it seems, did not agree with my encouragement to construct critical readings as part of the practice of everyday life.

Kate also did not get much out of the *I Like It Like That* exercise that I described in chapter 3:

A little racial. Price favored beautiful woman over intelligence, but she talked him into changing his mind. Stood up for herself and women in the Bronx. (first viewing critical reactions)

I liked how the latino girl stuck up for herself throughout the clip. In the beginning, male dominance in gender roles was shown. However, later the lady took over the power. Price immediately put down the woman and that bothered me. Lizette demonstrated the intelligence needed to improve her image as a woman. Price was also critical of her as living in the Bronx, stereotyping the neighborhood. Furthermore, when he saw "she was a hustler," he offered her a job. (second viewing critical reactions)

Obviously there are unbalanced gender roles for Lizette. She is disrespected until she proves her intelligence despite the fact she lives in the Bronx. (third viewing critical reactions)

Although Kate gives more complete descriptions—utilizing sociological terminology—of her reactions in the second and third readings, there is not much qualitative difference in the change in reception. In fact, on the second reading she notes that "I really did not notice any differences from last time ☹," and on the third reading she says that she has "No change from last time ☹." Both times she used a common doodle for disappointment, perhaps referencing her perception of my own response.

Kate's very last posting in the EC (week 15 coffee house) is a little more encouraging:

Because I had never been exposed to a class that revolved around discussion, I felt uncomfortable expressing my opinion aloud, however, after taking this class, I am prepared for another open discussion class. Although I did not participate [in inclass discussion], my mind was definitely working. I think of all my classes this semester, this class stimulated my mind the most as I now analyze products of the media I never thought was possible. I think Walt had a very unique style of teaching that kept my attention. I also found people's opinions altering mine as I thought about things more carefully.

Again, however, Kate is part of that group of students who will do what is necessary to get a good grade in a class and then will probably forget the lessons over the semester break. This would be disheartening in any manifestation, but it is especially so when the student is a freshman learning the college game. So while she did get something out of the class, I don't think she'll deploy critical literacy outside of class contexts, as does Dana, the subject of the next student spotlight box. Of course, there's always a chance that I can be wrong, though. I hope that I am.

Space Traders in the Spring

This class's atmosphere is much more comfortable than the other. Maybe it's the less freshmen effect. The last class may have been less comfortable due to their being green to college. (Anna FN, February 9)

This class is full of idealism. (Jennifer FN, February 9)

The *Space Traders* vote went pretty great! Several people responded with diverse, well thought-out answers. As always, though, there are comments that are surprising, such as a couple of people saying that racism is not an issue. (Jennifer FN, February 9)

As usual, we were all over the place today: mixing theories, experiences, and representations. (Walt FN, February 9)

As can be gleaned from just a small set of field notes, I was much more pleased with the critical literacy of the spring class than I was with the fall class. As suggested by Anna's field note, this was partly due to the composition of each class. As noted earlier, the fall class was composed primarily of freshmen and sophomores while the spring class was heavily populated by upperclassmen,[3] so the spring class's engagement was influenced by the older students' greater awareness of the norms of the Academy and (for some) the willingness to attempt to subvert those norms (many of their academically weaker peers have dropped out by this time).

As was the case in the fall, in the spring there was a previous incident that affected class engagement with *Space Traders*. It occurred on the Monday before the Wednesday screening, and is captured in Jennifer's postclass reflections from the next day (February 3):

Just briefly, for now, I will reflect upon the Virtual President/Prodigy video "Smack My Bitch Up." The class seemed to enjoy the "humor" of the VP clip as well as the nudity (censored) of the video. The main issue of concern was censorship. This seemed to be the only issue the class was concerned about, minus Bernice, who was disturbed by the clip's references to domestic violence in a humorous fashion.

I've made no secret about my opinions on this. I was offended from the first sentence on. "Every 30 seconds a bitch is slapped up" is not funny to me.

Considering I am a feminist activist, I was actually disturbed by this clip, enough to make me shed a couple of tears. I also happened to be in a pretty upset state from listening to the numerous anti-woman comments courtesy of the three misogynists behind me. However, I have recovered pretty much from this incident, though I am still a bit reserved about returning to class.

The topic of the class was gender and sexuality, and as part of the illustration of gendered representations in media I showed the class a clip of the rock group Prodigy's controversial video "Smack My Bitch Up," concerning abusive relationships. The particular clip I screened was part of an MTV program called *Virtual Bill,* which featured an animated President Bill Clinton introducing videos with humorous one-liners, and commenting on the videos while in progress (similar to the infamous program *Beavis and Butthead,* also an MTV production). Virtual Bill introduced the Prodigy video with commentary on "bitch slapping" as a national epidemic that he has vowed to fight to the fullest extent possible. As part of this speech, every other sentence seemed to include the word "bitch."

The class's response to Virtual Bill and the video itself, however, was more diverse than Jennifer's notes indicate. For instance, while Bernice was the most vocal about the humorous portrayal of domestic violence (sharing an account of personal experience with domestic abuse), several other women were vocal about it as well, including one woman who argued passionately that the portrayal was not offensive at all. Also, several men were active in the debate, from a plethora of perspectives, including censorship (of language as well as nudity).

The point to consider here is the "objectivity" issue of ethnography, leading to two points concerning autoethnography. Many would consider Jennifer's data to be tainted or biased, but I argue that by exploring the author's own deeply held perspectives in the field, autoethnography sheds insight into aspects of postmodern conditions of life. First, as there was researcher triangulation (Janesick 1994) I was able to record perspectives that Jennifer missed, and vice versa. We combined different slices of interpretations to form more expansive views. Second, and more important, an engagement with a researcher's own interests and feelings had a positive impact on the site as a whole, as was the case when Beeta and I reflexively analyzed our frustrations in the fall. Before screening *Space Traders* on Wednesday I told the class that while we should feel free to voice our perspectives, even if unpopular and/or disturbing, we should try to do so in as amicable a manner as possible (e.g., refrain from overtly vulgar expressions). One of the "three misogynists" approached me and thought he was being singled out and punished for his views. Specifically, he thought that Jennifer's observations of him would affect his grade, and, perhaps, outside activities if Jennifer and I contacted his employer (he worked in the public service sector). I told him that this was not the case and reassured him throughout the rest of the semester. Though he was less vocal for a couple of weeks after the discussion of the Prodigy video, he eventually regained his in-class intensity and passion. He and Jennifer (and she and the other two as well) also developed more multisided understandings over the semester, and established friendly rapport.

A slightly different version of the second concern was highlighted during the discussion of *Space Traders*:

Walt explains his phobia [of the number thirteen]. Him sharing stories like that helps students feel more comfortable sharing too. He is less sober and scholarly than he was at the start of the last semester. (Anna FN, February 9)

The mood of the class seemed overall pleasant. I felt very comfortable with these students. . . . Class seemed very receptive to Walt. (Jennifer FN, January 12, first day of class)

As discussed in the previous chapter, I shared personal stories and experiences throughout both semesters. In the spring semester, however, I was more at ease in this process, from the first day of class. This is due to two reasons. First, as this was my second time teaching s101 some of the bugs of a new course preparation were worked out; I was able to relax more as I had a general idea of where to place stories and how they would be received. Second, I could experiment with the class more as a certain pressure of collecting "good" data was lifted. Originally I had planned to only observe the fall class, so in a sense data collected in the spring were "bonus" data, and if I screwed up things it wouldn't be that big of a loss. As indicated earlier, however, I've come to formulate the inclusion of risky, personally "biased" data as part of good autoethnography.

Thinking about the teacher as text strategy, we see that it was more effective in the spring given that I had a larger base of experiences and knowledges to work with: I was able to help students consider implications of fragments of their experiences, and integrate them into a more critical perceptual framework. For instance, many made connections to lessons learned in other contexts:

Would it be easier to just let the African Americans go to space? Although this predicament is just a story, history suggests that the blacks would go. That's the type of environment we choose to live in. Even Tibetans have violence in their history. (EC response, coffee house)

The movie is very shocking. I think the government sort of dodged the decision themselves by setting up 800 numbers and telling the people to cast a vote. The media made the people really scared, or believe "Hey this is a good thing, look at LA, it is all clean now." Everyone and everybody will be just fine . . . until we want your blonde babies. (EC response, coffee house)

In my race and ethnic issues class we were discussing how many middle to upper-class white people ages 40+ are so secluded in their "white" world because of their job, neighborhood, friends, etc. that the only thing they see of the black community is what is shown on television, which is many times negative. (EC response, debate house)

I don't think the stereotype of heavy consumers of alcohol is right. It is how media and ads have made it out to be. Back home there is a neighborhood that is made up mostly of minorities. You don't see billboards for Cheetos or the next concert in town. All you see is either alcohol ads (always a Colt .45 ad somewhere) or cigarettes. (EC response, debate house)

The most disturbing part of the film was the very end when the caucasian anchorman gave the news report and you could see his sinister smile breaking through. Not only did the film hold stereotypes of African-Americans, but caucasians as well. (EC response, debate house)

I thought the portrayal of interracial relationships in *Space Traders* was interesting. The son's girlfriend or wife was white and she never said one single thing to anyone about the whole trade. She was just a little puppy dog. The son wasn't much better because he didn't seem worried about the whole trade until the day of it. He was dating a white girl, so he must not be a true black man. It seemed like it was sending a very negative message about inter-racial relationships. No one talked to the white girl, nor she to anyone else. It was like she was just there. They could have just as easily had a black couple or even a white girl that was involved in the fight against the trade and discussions about it. The son could have been more active and concerned. The two of them could have talked about the trade. Instead it just showed that inter-racial couples are just about holding hands and watching TV together. I was just curious to what other people thought about the film's portrayal of inter-racial couples. (EC response, coffee house)

The first two responses are from students who were in one of my previous s335 race and ethnic relations classes. I had also screened *Space Traders* then, so they were applying lessons learned to their second viewing.[4] The third response was from a student who was concurrently enrolled in s335, taught by a different instructor. Throughout this class she made connections with s335, such as the operation of "whiteness," the privileges that whites enjoy because of racial designations, but usually refuse to acknowledge (Frankenberg 1997; Hill 2004, 1997; Wray and Newitz 1997). The fourth and fifth responses make references to nonclass experiences. The author of the fifth posting was one of four nonwhites in the class, and would from time to time made arguments about difficulties of race that the white students were more reluctant to explore. A white student did examine the difficulties in the last response. It is noteworthy here that she was in an interracial relationship, so she has a certain self-interest that may have stopped full entry into the matrix of domination.

Note that I have included notation about the specific places that the messages were posted. The coffee house was an unstructured forum where students could post whatever they wanted, whereas the debate house centered on a specific question. To an extent, the more sophisticated answers posted in the spring versus the fall could be due to the questions posed:

On October 30, 1938, the nationwide radio broadcast of "The War of the Worlds" caused thousands to believe that Earth was under actual attack from Mars. As a result, many modern TV programs carry a warning message that the events depicted are not real. Do you think that a *Space Traders*-type program or series of programs should be broadcasted nationally in an effort to seriously kick-start a national conversation on race? Should warning labels be attached, or should we be led to believe that the events are "real"? (fall question, posted by me)

As viewed in the film, methods such as looking at African-American entertainment figures and sports stars as representatives of minority contributions to society were prominently seen as a humanitarian reason to stop the trade. A reason which showed the commercial benefits of stopping the trade focused on the issue that African Americans are one of the highest consumers of alcohol. Both of these portrayals were heavily enforced as the norms of society in the film. First of all, is the *Space Traders* version of the media portrayal of African Americans in society the same or similar to the current media's depiction of them? And, if so, do you believe that these portrayals are based on stereotypes, as we discussed Wednesday in class? Or do you think that these portrayals are reflections of what many see is currently happening in the African-American community? Why do you feel as you do? (spring question, posted by Jennifer)

Jennifer also added a reminder about critical literacy: "Don't let the pressures of political correctness hold you back in this question. This question allows for a lot of opinions. Don't be afraid to dig into the complexities hidden behind this issue. I think we can hammer out a pretty great discussion." So, obviously, our instructions affect quality of responses, but the nuanced thoughts that were also expressed in the coffee house suggest that another factor was the general higher level of engagement of the spring class.

As was the case in the fall class, the spring class was more active outside of class than in the class discussions: there were twenty-eight EC postings (twelve in the debate house, and sixteen in the coffee house), and eight students chose the *Space Traders* option for essay 2 (the other option was to analyze "the circuit of culture" of a media product; in the fall everyone was required to discuss *Space Traders*). As previously noted, however, they did generate interesting and thoughtful discussion in class, to a higher level than in the fall class. For instance, I also conducted the anonymous ballot concerning the state of a present-day trade with the spring class. This time around I got thirteen "yes" votes (up from the two votes in the fall), although none would publicly identify themselves. This did, however, prompt an impassioned speech by one of the students who was disturbed by the mock vote, and several responses to the vote (and the speech) in the coffee house, such as "I thought that the whole concept of the *Space Traders* video was very thought-provoking. It made me think quite honestly about race relations in today's society. I would like to think that we are a completely civilized society that would think such an idea was outrageous, but I was shocked to see some of the responses in the mock vote in class on 2–9–98."

The spring class was also more candid in discussions of issues other than race, given that their instructor is African American. Jennifer noted that "I think that the lack of racial diversity in the class really does speak loudly when it comes to discussing *Space Traders*. People don't seem to have too many diverse opinions about race" (FN, February 9). In the introduction to *White Trash*, Wray and Newitz (1997:6) argue that "[A] great deal of work still needs to be done before multiculturalism—and whites' participation in it—is associated with a progressive, interracial political strategy rather than a victim chic and racial divisiveness." Anna noted that "overall this class seems to be more interested and more engaged than the last class. It is closer to the class dynamic we had in s335 [which was 40 percent minority]" (FN, February 9). As expected, the more diverse the public sphere, the greater the willingness to explore transformative multiculturalism.

As noted throughout, however, the spring class did engage in critical thought about race and other issues more than the fall class, even if not quite at the level of my "race and ethnic relations" classes. More important, they began to see the significance of considering the implications of intertextual articulations:

I thought *Space Traders* was interesting and quite disturbing at the same time. It makes you think about how the majority populations really think about minorities. Have things really changed that much sense the times of segregation and the fight for civil rights, or are feelings now just kept on the down low until something comes up? You never know, and a film like this makes you think could something like that ever happen? Obviously not the alien part, but would our country basically take out a minority group for great economic gain. I don't know the answer to that. I hope the answer is no. (EC response, coffee house)

Growing up kind of sheltered I guess I didn't know that this feeling of our world being so white powered was real. . . . I walked out of class, upset with what I saw and I called my Dad. (media journal entry)

I do not believe that our media portrays the African Americans to be just sports figures and beer drinkers. It is so hard for me to say because until I took this class I just really don't notice black, white, whatever, when I am watching a commercial or reading an ad, I just see people. So I personally think that the media just show everyone alike. I am beginning to change my mind about that now though since being in this class, I've been actually searching to see if there is a particular image trying to be displayed in an ad. (EC response, debate house)

Space Traders was one of the most shocking and thought-provoking pieces of media that I have seen. After watching the movie in class, I told many of my friends about it and discussed many avenues and implications that the movie had made. (essay response)

Indeed, *Space Traders* is a very polysemic text that invokes multiple interpretations. I made the text strange, helping students investigate occluded meanings and effaced articulations. The overt racial aspects of the text itself, however, work to dampen some of the possible understandings. I will close this chapter with a brief analysis of one of the more "neutral" strange texts I deployed in the effort to create the college classroom as Pensieve.

Dana—"successful" intervention

I was really frustrated in class when we talked about [the McDonald's place mat; see Figure 3.2] as possibly holding racial connotations. Personally, I think this is just a hamburger ad that has no racial undertones. I get really annoyed when everything needs to have a deeper meaning. Maybe the producers of this ad made other ads with big pictures of minorities . . . does that mean it is derogatory towards whites? I'm sorry if this sounds harsh or unfair, maybe I would see things differently if I were a minority, but really I'm just tired of the term "racism" being thrown around like a loose term. Racism is in fact a strong word which should be thought long and hard about before it is used as a label. Why can't we just all get along? —WEEK 5 POSTING BY DANA in the spring image house

One of the most rewarding aspects of the attempt to create Pensieves is when students enter the matrix of domination to examine intersections of the social determinants of their experiences and biographies. Dana—a junior in the spring class—was one such student. As suggested by her posting, she initially resisted entry (she also wrote in her media journal that "I understand that [*Space Traders*] is trying to make the point that all whites hate black people (whatever!!)"), but by the end of the class she was looking at issues much more sociologically.

Consider her later postings in the EC, which were mostly in the reflect house, where students visited and commented on World Wide Web sites. In week 13 the spring semester students visited "Vagrant Gaze," in which homeless men were given cameras to document their lives. The author of the first posting about this site argued that she thought the site glorified homelessness and encouraged people to take "the easy way out" of their problems. Dana seconded a response that homelessness was not necessarily a choice, adding that "I think the camera gives the homeless a voice they don't normally have." The following week the students visited "siren.org," a site listing the interests and products of a (then) fifteen-year-old teenage girl. Dana was among the minority to dispute postings that the site was excessively narcissistic, arguing that "it may be immature to some, but she's fifteen years old, and for that age I think she's quite mature, especially with all her accomplishments and goals in life."

Dana was one of the few students who had seen *I Like It Like That* before I showed the seven-minute clip to the class. While on the second in-class reading she indicated that she had "no change [in critical reactions] from the last time I saw it," she did develop a sociological analysis to differentiate her pre-class experience and the first in-class reading:

This film is analyzing the different social structures of racial classes. The white record producer is a naive man who has asserted his knowledge of money over everything else. Lisette is a smart, outspoken lower class Puerto Rican who knows about music but isn't given the chance to prove it, solely because of her race and social standing. (first viewing critical reactions)

I respect Lisette for standing up to the white producer now, more than I did the first time I saw the film. Before I just saw her as annoying and star-crazy. (change in critical reactions, first in-class reading)

Turning to the media journal, Dana made several errors in the discussion of concepts and theories in the first set of six entries: she incorrectly used intertextuality, the matrix of domination, the sociological imagination, and hegemony. In the second set of entries, she had corrected the errors and took chances to explore new concepts as well (such as sampling, narrowcasting, and audience reception). Most students, on the other hand, stuck with the same concepts once I indicated that they were using them correctly. Thus, it seems that Dana took me up on constant appeals for students to push the envelope and continually explore new topics and ideas, even if they did not fully grasp them the first time out.

In chapter 6 I explore the use of weekly salon about the TV show *The X-Files* to gauge if and how students are using media literacy concepts after completing their s101 class. Along with the students of the chapter 3 spotlight boxes, Dana was a participant. She extensively used concepts from s101 in the meetings, and told me that she encouraged her sorority sisters to analyze the show critically. Perhaps most notably, she initiated discussion about the racial representation of certain characters, including one whom I did not think to critique. She has, indeed, come a long way from the "Why can't we just all get along" (by ignoring race) of the image house posting about the McDonald's place mat.

Dana, then, is a "successful" intervention in several ways: she learned to enter the matrix of domination, was willing to continually explore new ideas in class assignments (though not always nailing them down; she earned a B+ in the class), and used course concepts outside of class. I am pleased that she got something out of the experience.

The "Post-Modern Prometheus" Unveiled

During the spring semester the class encountered an episode of the TV show *The X-Files* the week after *Space Traders*. *The X-Files* is about the adventures of two FBI agents—Fox Mulder and Dana Scully—who battle the paranormal, extraterrestrial aliens, and vast government conspiracies. On Monday, February 16, I showed the class the sixty-minute episode "Post-Modern Prometheus" (Carter 1997), fast-forwarding through commercials. We had a brief discussion of the show afterwards, and more extensive analysis during the next class (on Wednesday).

The episode originally aired on November 30, 1997, so it was still in the memories of a few students. Jennifer and I enjoyed it as well, as Jennifer notes that "Oh, how much I do love seeing this episode again! It is my favorite!" (FN, February 16). It was also enjoyed by first-time viewers, even though it could (and did) disturb some, due to elements that hit very close to (a literal) home. The following summary of the episode is taken from the official *X-Files* web site (http://www.thex-files.com/), and has the header "Townspeople in rural Indiana believe a Frankenstein-like creature roams the countryside."

In a rural Indiana neighborhood, Shaineh Berkowitz watches a daytime talk show on television. So entranced is she by the interview, that she fails to notice someone covering the home with termite tenting. A dark figure enters the kitchen and drops a white cake into a skillet, triggering a chemical reaction that produces a gaseous white cloud. Sensing a presence in the house, Shaineh investigates. Suddenly, a horribly disfigured, Frankenstein-like face emerges from the misty darkness. Shaineh gasps in horror.

Later, as the agents drive through the Indiana farmland, Scully reads aloud a letter addressed to Mulder. In it, Shaineh describes how, eighteen years earlier, a presence entered her smoke-filled bedroom as, strangely, the voice of singer Cher filled the air. Three days later she woke up pregnant with her son, Izzy. Shaineh explains that she saw Mulder on "The Jerry Springer Show," and hopes he will investigate her case. The agents do, indeed, drive to Shaineh's home. There they discover a comic book bearing the exact likeness of the creature Shaineh claims attacked her. Shaineh explains the monster is called The Great Mutato, a creation of Izzy's fertile imagination. Izzy claims he, and many others in the community, have seen the creature—who apparently has a penchant for peanut butter sandwiches. Izzy and his friends lead the detectives to a wooded area, and using sandwiches for bait, lure the creature from its hiding place. The group gives chase, but the creature disappears into the darkness. Mulder then encounters an Old Man, who claims the real monster is his own son, renowned scientist Dr. Francis Pollidori. The agents visit Pollidori, who describes his experiments in genetic manipulation. He displays a photo of a fruit fly head . . . with legs growing out of its mouth. Later, Pollidori bids goodbye to his wife, Elizabeth, as he embarks on a trip out of town. Moments later, termite tenting falls past Elizabeth's window.

When the agents stop by a country diner in downtown Bloomington, they are feted with heaping plates of food. It turns out that the entire town believes Jerry Springer will do a story on the creature . . . the result of a newspaper article in which Mulder is quoted as verifying the monster's existence. The agents realize Izzy secretly tape recorded their conversations.

As the agents drive along a country road, Mulder spots Pollidori's tented house. The pair race inside, where they discover Elizabeth's unconscious body. Shortly thereafter, the agents also lose consciousness. The Old Man, Professor Pollidori's father, steps from the smoke, a gas mask covering his face. When the agents regain consciousness, Elizabeth describes her attacker as a hideously deformed man with two mouths.

The Old Man brings the Creature a peanut butter sandwich as it watches the movie *Mask*, starring Cher, on television. Pollidori confronts his father, and in a rage, strangles him.

A mob of townspeople forms around the local post office as a mail clerk proclaims he's found the monster. He pulls someone wearing a rubber Mutato mask from the back room, then yanks off the mask, exposing Izzy. The postal worker then displays a box he intercepted, which is filled with identical masks.

Records indicate that the residue from the white cakes is a substance used to anesthetize herds of animals. Its use is monitored by the FDA, leading the agents back to the Old Man's farm. When the agents arrive at the scene, a diligent newspaper girl, who had been recording notes about the case, describes how she witnessed the creature burying the Old Man. Shortly thereafter, an angry mob makes its way towards the farm. The agents realize Pollidori killed his father. They befriend the frightened Mutato and attempt to escape, but they are spotted by the mob and retreat into a cellar. Pollidori and the townspeople burst into the basement. There, Pollidori claims the Creature was brought to life by his father. The Creature claims he never harmed another soul. He explains how, 25 years earlier, the Old Man realized his son was conducting secret experiments—of which he (Mutato) was an unfortunate product. The Old Man grew to love the Creature, and then set out to create it a mate. As the Creature continues his tale, the agents, putting together two and two, look around the cellar at the townspeople . . . one of whom resembles a horse, another a Billy goat and so on. The mob concludes Mutato is not a monster after all. A police cruiser transports Pollidori from the scene. The agents take the Creature into custody, but instead of transporting him to jail, they head for a Memphis nightclub, where Cher sings to Mutato, her biggest fan.

Although this web site description identifies the location of the episode as being in Bloomington, Indiana, that is not at all clear in the episode itself. In fact, one must deduce the location from three clues, each only briefly shown in passing: (1) license plates on cars are Indiana plates, (2) the agents show Pollidori a "University of Indiana Press" news release, and (3) Mulder reads a "Bloomington World" newspaper in the coffee shop. On Wednesday I asked the class if anyone thought about where the episode may be set, and one student identified Bloomington, and cited clues (2) and (3). This set off a spirited debate about stereotypes in class, as well as in the EC:

I think that the show was taking a shot at Indiana as a whole. It was inferring that rural people (or white trash) think shows like "Jerry Springer" are the watchdogs of America. That talk shows are responsible news reporting agencies. This of course makes a statement about the intelligence of said rurals. It also offered some insight into the compassion country folk are capable of. Although that is definitely a secondary point of the authors!

the x-files episode viewed in class this week is one that stuck with me for quite a while after the first time that it aired. i do agree with many of the other comments made that it portrays small towns in a very negative way, but there are some people that exist just as shown on this episode. i believe that they were trying to show the extremes/rednecks to make people more aware that this mentality is still alive. this episode was extremely moving, and it showed that so-called "freaks" have hearts, emotions, and should be loved not feared, hated, or treated like nothing.

After sitting and listening to our discussion in class about white trash individuals I felt other races were left out of this stereotyping. I happen to come across an episode of the "Simpsons" and Milhouse said to Bart, "Well, you're nothing but yellow trash!" That made me question why white trash is confined to whites only. Is there such a think as Black trash or Asian Trash? In reality there is, we just don't label it. Since many portrayals of minorities in the media are not the most positive of sorts networks may deem it necessary to poke the fun stick at someone else—the shrinking majority.

I am a big fan of the x-files because I think it is a smart show that has very interesting stories and just weird stuff that's pretty cool, it gives things a new perspective. I thought the modern day prometheus episode was cool, and a good commentary on society. When large groups of people get together, they seem to exaggerate things and jump to conclusions, not to mention following a leader who's intentions are a little questionable and could be self-serving . . . just take a look at Hitler. True the episode was supposed to take place in Bloomington, and the town was small minded, but that was the beauty of it. It was supposed to be Pulp Fiction, and I'm not talking about the Quentin Tarantino movie either. I mean, in the one of the final scenes when they have the Great Mutato cornered and it flashes from the townspeople to the barnyard animals they resemble, that is saying that we all really live in a great big barnyard and WE ARE THE ANIMALS. Nature plays a part in the world of humankind and society, with everyone playing their little role in the environment so it can come together and be a functional whole. When you mess with nature and something foreign is introduced into your environment, something you can't understand, you naturally are scared of it and want to remove or destroy it. It was also supposed to have a comical twist, with quick wit but a plot that still makes you think. I think that's what we need more of, shows that actually make you think instead of turning your brain into a virtual jello mold because you stare at a television screen for countless hours a day and absorb what amounts in reality to, well, crap.

Notice the intertextuality expressed in the postings, with references to the TV shows *The Simpsons* and *The Jerry Springer Show,* and the movie *Pulp Fiction.* Other media products referenced in-class and in the EC include comic books, the TV show *The Beverly Hillbillies,* an interview with actor Tom Arnold, and various interviews and products featuring the stars of *The X-Files.* McLaughlin (1996:153) argues that students "have experienced a culture that values image over reality, that has replaced production with information, that has developed a popular culture of intricate semiotic sophistication and technical virtuosity, that deploys spectacular signs, that encourages the creation of personal identity within those sign systems—that is, they have lived the postmodern, and they are adept at reading its artifacts." Through exposure to strange texts like *Space Traders* and *The X-Files,* and a discussion of sociological concepts and theories (such as the sociological imagination, hegemony, ethnographic reception, and whiteness), I was able to help transform their vernacular understanding of popular media into critical agency about interaction of personal understandings and larger social structures. Jennifer notes that "Walt's reference to popular culture really hit everyone. People get so used to seeing things on television and in films that they don't realize the extent of its integration into their lives and perceptions" (FN, February 16).

The concept of "whiteness" is one underexamined aspect of many students' lives. In our discussions of "Post-Modern Prometheus" we explored the "second wave" of whiteness. The "first wave" focused on making whiteness visible, marking it as a social construction that is impermanent and situated; these studies demonstrated that whiteness matters, that whites have privileges due solely to their racial categorization (e.g., see Frankenberg 1993; Morrison 1992). "Second wave" writings (see Jacobs 1997) move on to examine *how* whiteness operates in conjunction with other social categories, issues, and powers: what are the ways it matters, and what are the consequences of particular articulations? In the introduction to *Whiteness,* Mike Hill (1997:12) adds that the second wave must not be surfed in such a way that recenters whiteness in "an attempt to 'lactify' ethnic differences and stay relevant in these lean, mean times of liquid cultural capital." Further, in post-9/11 America strategies should be created to reduce whiteness's power to terrorize; whiteness should be critically interrogated "to explore the remnants of white identity as a way of mobilizing one's democratic commitments within what might be called (a little awkwardly, I realize) an economy of absence" (Hill 2004:8).

In class I explicitly called whiteness to the floor, by asking "What does this episode say about white people?" After a minute of blank stares, one of the students from a rural background raised his hand and made points that he expanded in the EC, the first of the previous citations. Other students then joined in, both from urban and rural backgrounds. They explored intersections of the standard race-class-gender triangle, as well as other concerns such as social segregation and aesthetics, as illustrated in these two EC postings, of which the main themes were initially voiced in class discussion:

Some aspects I found interesting about the show was the fact that it was in black and white and that it played off of old horror movie ideas. . . . I think that they try to create as much atmosphere in each episode to make the show more interesting and keep their viewers guessing as to what they are going to do next. This is also a quality that I admire most about the show, they pay so much attention to small details to which makes you pay more attention to what is happening so you can pick up on small aspects such as the fact that it was in Indiana.

I think the term white trash was created by other whites who felt intellectually and socially above people within their same race. I'm from New York and inside the city limits that term is used to stereotype homeless, poor people, and drug addicts.

Additionally, in the EC students explored intersections of whiteness with Queer Theory, the study of the political and social poetics and problematics involved in the social construction of complex (homo)sexuality.[5] This started when a student, Laura, concluded an EC post with "[White trash] is not a concrete concept with an exact definition. It is not like being gay." I posted a response that "Laura raises a very interesting point in the last post: 'White Trash' is not concrete like being gay. Let me turn that into two questions for us to think about. One, is being a gay man or lesbian concrete, that is, does everyone know and agree about what those things 'are'? Two, while using 'white trash' may be a stretch because of the pejorative 'trash,' can the somewhat similar terms 'hillbilly' and 'redneck' be used in positive ways? And to connect the two questions, what's the role of media in this reappropriation, the process of giving a term a different meaning and use?" Several students joined the discussion, with very insightful observations:

I agree with what Laura said about the difference between self-labeling yourself as "queer" and "white trash." They are two completely different things. First of all, there's not clear definition of what white trash is. I don't think someone would want to label themselves as "trash." I realize that neither label (queer or white trash) says anything about their morality. By homosexuals embracing this name, it just let other people know they were not bothered by being called queer—that that is not something they are ashamed of. I don't see how this could be applied to white trash—how people could turn the term around to mean something positive, something they are proud of. People are not trash!!!!

One may claim to be proud of being a hillbilly, or even a redneck because the term isn't seen as negative to everyone. Remember the "Beverly Hillbillies"? They were portrayed as a good old fashioned, wholesome family. Society didn't look down on them despite their "hillbilly" status. But, the term "white trash" is different. All of society connects it with being lazy, dirty, poor, and immoral. That is why no one categorizes themselves as "white trash." But, many think of hillbillies as just people living on a small farm raising pigs to keep from the rich lifestyle, not necessarily as immoral bums.

I don't think there is anything concrete. I have known men and women that "like" their own sex, but wouldn't date one. Some of them thought themselves as gay, others bi, others straight. I don't think those terms have a concrete meaning at all. Back in high school we did a story on rednecks. The people we wrote about called themselves rednecks, without the writers first labeling them. Everyone got a kick out of the story. Anyway, it is the context I think that determines if one is using redneck or hillbilly as a put-down. If you are calling yourself one, you might be proud of your background. If someone is calling someone else a redneck, it probably isn't exactly to place blessings on them! Media is part of the problem with multiple meanings. Some movie, article, or song will put a new spin on the word, possibly make it the opposite of what it was (derogatory to "compliment" and vice versa) and cause the questioning of its future use.

A note on the first citation: the student was responding more to a brief allusion Laura made in class, rather than to my posting. Once again, full flowering of thought bloomed in the EC. This is to be expected, given that students need time and energy to ponder and assimilate multiple fragments introduced in class. Thought and debate were, however, very much engaged in class itself, more than in either of the *Space Traders* discussion days. This should also be expected, given that the text was "neutral," that it did not have any explicit comment on a social category of which the instructor was perceived to have a strong investment. Since I am not "white," students felt more comfortable exploring this social construction; it was my job to push the discussion into second-wave whiteness territory, exploring complicated issues and implications instead of the easy, dismissive comments that started out the discussion:

I think the term white trash is just classism at work. It's not good enough to stop at minorities, you've got to find a way to make yourself better against other whites. I think there's already enough negative stereotypes for minorities, so there needs to be some for whites now. I couldn't believe how people were laughing when someone said something about living in a trailer, much less someone being homeless. The term white trash is horrible—because someone enjoys trapping animals and lives in a trailer does not mean they are just throwaways. Like the guy in class said, his cousin may not be the most productive member of society, but I think his honesty is much more of a contribution to society. (EC response)

As demonstrated, by the end of the period students were thinking more critically about issues like whiteness, stereotypes, and intertextuality, and went to the EC to explore some of their ideas. Some of the active students—like Laura, and another student who said he liked being called a "hick"—had not been very active in class to that point, so it was doubly gratifying to see new students coming to voice. bell hooks (1994a:41) writes that "to hear each other (the sound of different voices), to listen to one another, is an exercise in recognition. It also ensures that no student remains invisible." In the classroom as Pensieve I want *all* my students to become visible, to engage in the tough but rewarding work of making articulations of personal experience and societal operation.

hooks (1994a:39) also argues that "the unwillingness to approach teaching from a standpoint that includes awareness of race, sex, and class is often rooted in the fear that classrooms will be uncontrollable, that emotions and passions will not be contained. . . . Making the classroom a democratic setting where everyone feels a responsibility to contribute is a central goal of transformative pedagogy." In order to create the classroom as Pensieve I called explicit attention to the forces of race, gender, class, and sexual orientation, and put my own passionate understandings and experiences on the table to help other students more critically explore their own. At the end of the spring discussion of "Post-Modern Prometheus" Jennifer wrote, "This discussion got pretty detailed and intricate. I was more impressed with the class's observations. The more and more I hear what these students have to say, the more impressed I become" (field note, February 18). Indeed, though the spring and fall classes differed in their approaches and extent of critical social agency, and reaction to the deployment of my teacher as text strategy, I was pleased with both classes' development over the semester. Exploring strange texts in and of Pensieves definitely has a key place in efforts to make postmodern conditions of social life more democratic and humane.

Chapter Five

Breaking and Making Frames as Context

On Monday I walked out in the hall just before class started. Walking back to class when I passed two older professors, one of whom had peeked into my classroom. He was saying that it "didn't have the right ambiance," that it was too laid-back for a serious class. I was playing Charlie Parker. Note earlier comment by one of two students when I started music as they were packing to leave previous class: "Wish I were in this class."
—WALT FIELD NOTE, February 18

I was personally interested from the beginning. I walked in, John Coltrane was playing, the atmosphere was right on. —First impressions assignment, spring semester

In order to create the college classroom as Pensieve, I use a number of unusual approaches and "strange texts," as we have seen in previous chapters. During the 1997–1998 autoethnography I played music before each class as another such technique to create an atmosphere in which students assembled fragments from disparate sources to form more multisided understandings of themselves and their social worlds. As suggested by my field note, some academics would scoff at such a move because they consider it as reducing the legitimacy of the class-room, making it cater more toward student whims and interests rather than engaging serious academic thought (see Aronowitz 2000; Dellucchi and Korgen 2002; Dellucchi and Smith 1997a, 1997b). Anderson and Irvine (1993:82), however, argue that critical literacy is "learning to read and write as part of the process of becoming conscious of one's experience as historically constructed within specific power relations," and that ethnographic practices can help in this effort. It is my task, then, to use whatever means are at my disposal to create contexts for active learning, even if that means breaking frames of acceptable behavior for some teachers.

As part of the autoethnography I would occasionally ask students to consider the ways in which our presence in a large lecture room at Indiana University in the year 1997 or 1998 affected our ideas and perspectives. In other words, the classroom itself became the text under study. In order to make the classroom a strange text (where usually hidden aspects were called into light) I experimented with alternative formats for conducting class. In each semester I included a "Storytelling Day," in which I read short stories from Saki (Williams 1978) to the class, to highlight and explore attention to several internal and external interpersonal dynamics. Additionally, in each semester I conducted "Kiva" sessions, in which I broke the class into small groups of students and had them meet me or an assistant at an on-campus restaurant for informal discussion. Each group met for an hour, in lieu of attending the regular seventy-five-minute class.

Unfortunately, as we go through this chapter we will see that I did not make these alternative formats strange enough. In the years after the autoethnography I created extensions of the techniques that more thoroughly helped students develop critical consciousness. I will explore these practices and other refinements in chapter 7.

Fall Storytelling

Cassie confided in me today that this class is "fuckin' weird." she's never had an unstructured class such as this . . . says all we do in here is "talk about shit . . . i mean, it's cool and all, but we actually do shit in my other classes . . . like take quizzes and shit . . . but i like this class . . . it's relaxing." (Beeta FN, October 8, very beginning of class)

It's amazing how field notes sometimes perfectly capture the right sentiment at the right moment. Not only did "Cassie's" remarks sum up part of the effort to create the classroom as Pensieve to that point, they anticipated the strange turn that class would take on that particular day. Originally the topic was "the news as global," but since the students seemed to be tiring of the recent focus on the production end of culture I decided to shift into the more exciting consumption side a day early. I must admit, I too was looking forward to the turn, so that made the decision that much easier.

Cassie's perspectives here mirror the articulation of the professors in this chapter's epigraph: if a class is laid-back, you can't be really doing anything important; talk is one thing, but action is another. I try to teach students that in late modern/postmodern conditions electronically mediated discourse is integral to the production of reality (Fiske 1994a, 1994b; Grossberg 1997a, 1997b; Kellner 2003, 1995a). "Media culture," Kellner (2003:1) adds, "not only takes up always-expanding amounts of time and energy, but also provides ever more material for fantasy, dreaming, modeling thought and behavior, and identities." I tell students that they should pay explicit attention to the contexts producing this condition, in order to better understand themselves and their surroundings. In this effort, storytelling days of the 1997–1998 autoethnography served three purposes: illustrated the operation of social formations, interrogated social stratification, and helped students come to voice.

John Fiske (1994b:192) makes this distinction between a "social formation" and a "social category":

A social category holds its members constantly within its conceptual grip; a social formation is formed and dissolved more fluidly, according to contextual conditions. It is identified by what members do rather than what they are, and as such is better able to account nonreductively for the complexities and contradictions of everyday life in a highly elaborated society.

Although, of course, one can endlessly debate semantics and put forth alternate understandings of social formations (see, e.g., Grossberg 1992), Fiske's main point is very pertinent for an analysis of storytelling day: students contextually create understandings of social issues and act in accordance with those perspectives, more so than in accordance with rigid transcendent understandings of concepts like "student" and "woman" and "man."

Take the formation of "men," for instance. I wanted the class—men and women—to think about the effects of dominant understandings of masculinity, that "men" don't do things that render them "weak" or "emotional," that they speak for others before they examine themselves (Connell 1995; Seidler 1989). Shortly into the day's discussion of Saki's "The Story-Teller" (Williams 1978) I asked a pointed question to the men: "would you read a story like this to other men?"[1] *All* the men whom I looked at (and it was most of the ten or so present that day) started to fidget and/or laugh nervously rather than respond. I then opened the discussion for all:

[Male student] says no, society would think that was weird. rob says reading stories could be looked upon as a socially intimate act . . . so between 2 guys, this seems wrong. (Beeta FN, October 8)

Girl says it's partly because men are competitive and don't like to have other men do things for them. (Lori FN, October 8)

good discussion following walt's question. girl in front row with long brown hair & glasses made good comments about socialization & women being more nourishing & what not. (Rob FN, October 8)

We talked about gender role socialization in general, and sketched ways in which social movements like feminism were changing our thoughts about "masculinity" and "femininity." Anna and Jennifer were particularly vocal and insightful in this stage of the discussion, which was not surprising given that they were two of the only three women who publicly called themselves "feminist." I then tried to make an articulation between gender roles and sexuality, as nicely summarized and explored in a couple of long field notes from Lori on October 8:

Clear that he's driving this conversation somewhere. Walt again asks question to men "what would you do if roommate approached you and wanted to read you a story?" Finally, he gets to his point by admitting that when his best friend 1st asked him, he thought he was being a "faggot." Adds that for most men there might be an element of homophobia, that he was able to work through his. Nervous laughter from class at faggot comment.

I usually try to guess where W. is going w/his points, but in this case I had no idea. I was actually surprised to hear him associate reading aloud with homophobia . . . maybe it's because of my gender or perhaps it's because I just don't think that way . . . because I suppose many women could have similar thoughts. Whatever the case, I do wonder why we as a class, myself included, found it ok to laugh at the faggot remark. I simply cannot imagine that had Walt been a white person using the notorious "N" word to make a point, there would have been such laughter. I think it would be different if the point Walt was trying to make was that it shouldn't matter one way or another if someone is gay or not. But instead, he seemed to be explaining that once he realized that straight men read aloud to one another too, it was then acceptable for him to do the same. Disclosing this seemed to be his way of telling guys in class that just because you read to another guy doesn't mean you're a "faggot." This, however, doesn't address real issue that it shouldn't matter whether someone is gay or not. I do often wonder whey it seems like its still socially acceptable to so casually make derogatory remarks about homosexuals. Even in this era of superficial political correctness, gays are still regarded as pretty open to blatant insults. WHY????

Lori introduces excellent points here, ones that we did not fully explore in class, and which were not made strange enough by me. Collins (1991) says that we often downplay our social advantages and focus on our disadvantages. In this case I was reluctant to interrogate my own heterosexual privilege to help others explore their own privilege and/ or disadvantage. Since I was disinclined to deploy the teacher as text strategy here I did not productively take the class into the matrix of domination regarding sexuality.

A significant part of that reluctance was an acceptance of an important traditional boundary of social inquiry, the question of appropriate subject matter. This was a class about "media," after all—I told myself— not "sexuality"; these issues are better dealt with in a class with a title like "Sexual Diversity." I should have been more reflexive, however, and realized that I could use issues of media influence in the social construction of sexuality to explore the larger category of sexuality itself. Indeed, I did this extensively with categories such as race, class, and gender, as we have seen in previous chapters. Why not with sexuality?

Once again, one reason was the reluctance to fully deploy the teacher as text technique through an exploration of the nuances of my own sexuality, an area to which I've devoted much less study than race, class, and gender.[2] I am, thus, not as comfortable with exposing it to others, especially as a tool for students to use. More important, however, when I discuss issues such as race, class, and gender there are always visible members of the Other present; in the fall class no one was "out," no one identified themselves as gay or lesbian. Although the presence of insiders doesn't necessarily eliminate essentialism (and, conversely, the absence of insiders does not necessarily guarantee essentialism), the teacher as text strategy works best when insiders interact with outsiders to question and discuss identities from a number of perspectives.

In previous chapters we have encountered evidence that students changed articulations of general social formations regarding race, class, and gender. The second reason I read Saki's "The Story-Teller" was to provide yet another exercise in the construction of the sociological imagination, to help students investigate how practices that seem to be totally private and personal—like reading—are, indeed, affected by larger social forces, such as social class membership. This is illustrated in one of Lori's field notes about the political correctness of certain terms and speech, as well as about the construction of orality itself:

I make point that act of reading aloud itself—in certain contexts—is a reflection of class privilege. Walt asks me to expand after putting "cultural capital" on board. I explain that historically oral cultures have emerged from illiterate groups, and that literacy and reading aloud have been regarded as symbols of high culture. (Lori FN, October 8)

that story walt read was . . . i don't know, i don't really understand why he chose to read it. was it because the class was so small today? i liked the story about white people smelling like dogs [when wet] better. (Rob FN, October 8)

Once again, Lori introduced a very pertinent and needed nuance into the discussion, which was further developed by the contributions of Beeta and Rob in the subsequent discussion. Rob's field note points to the third reason that I read the story to the class: I wanted to encourage students to come to voice, to make their own articulations of personal troubles and societal issues. After telling them one of my own stories to get things rolling (I did not personally know any white people until eleventh grade, at which time a white student came to my high school and was placed in my homeroom; after the first day of rain I surreptitiously smelled him to see if the stereotype was true), several students relayed their own.

Two interesting points emerged from the discussion arising out of the stories, which closed out the class period. First, two of the three story authors were women who did not normally speak in class ("Cassie" was one), and many of the respondents also were not my "regular" talkers.[3] This suggests that the personal storytelling experiment was, indeed, successful in helping some come to voice. Second, the discussion got at larger sociological dynamics that affected their experiences, such as issues of the power of place on articulation. Cassie's story involved a "fogger," a machine for spreading pesticides to keep dust down on unpaved country roads. I used another student's request for clarification of the term to launch into an investigation of perspectives on rural life in general. Students from small towns animatedly responded that they resented being termed "hicks"; some specifically argued that just because their towns were racist, that does not make them racist as well. At this point the period was almost at an end so I stated that we'd revisit those points next week, specifically saying that while it's important to avoid and reject unfounded stereotypes, we could and should explore sociological generalizations about connections of experiences and structures.

No one, however, referenced specific class topics and dynamics of the day in the EC or in assignments, so I can't generalize to form larger significances here. Unfortunately, the same thing happened in the spring semester as well.

Spring Storytelling

Today was storytelling day. It went overall very well, considering many do not know exactly how to take this alternative form of media. (Jennifer FN, March 9)

I started out the spring 1998 storytelling session by asking the students how many people read short stories. Only about a third of the class raised their hands. I also asked the fall class this question and, similarly, about a third of that class raised their hands, too. There was a different response to the next question: "How many read aloud to another person?" Three people in the spring class raised their hands for this, while in the fall class only one person answered affirmatively, and that was Beeta.

The spring class's reaction during the reading of the story (Saki's "The Lumber-Room," about a child who outsmarts adult caretakers) was also slightly different from the fall class's reaction. In the fall the class laughed only at a (I think) quite funny story when I broke frame and looked up at the class, laughing myself. In the spring the class laughed in a few spots on its own (such as when main character Nicholas called his aunt "the Evil One"). Once again, this is largely the result of the fall class looking more to me for cues about how to behave in new situations.

Neither the fall class nor the spring class took up any of the issues raised on storytelling days in the EC or future assignments. I suspect, however, that the spring class's noncontinuation was due to a combination of ongoing debate about issues raised in the previous week's Kiva sessions (detailed later), and winding down in anticipation of the next week's spring break. My sense of the fall class's reluctance to continue the discussion was more related to being overwhelmed with topics that go to the core of their young (in terms of chronological age) identities. I cannot rise much above the level of speculation here, however, without any supporting triangulated data.

I do have data on two other differences between the semesters regarding storytelling day. First, recall that the spring class had students who read to others regularly. These students introduced an important consideration into the discussion, that storytelling can be an important and pleasurable shared activity in and of itself, rather than a means of conveying information, as many of the students had regarded oral communication, especially one student who asked "what possible reason could I have for reading a story to someone?" (Walt FN, March 9). The three students (one woman, two men; all older students [late twenties–early forties]) who read to each other all shared tales of how their bonds to their partners were strengthened through reading stories (even novels) aloud. They also related perspectives as shared and summed by Anna, in a March 9 field note taken while I read the story:

I start thinking about how reading out loud gives the reader a chance to have people listen attentively to what they are saying. I really enjoy when people listen to me attentively, but it doesn't happen often enough in normal conversation. People are too busy thinking of what to say in contribution to the conversation. When someone is reading to you you have to save comments for the end and you can't drift off much into your own thoughts or you will lose track of what is happening. I think I should read out loud to some friends. I would dig it and I think it would be fun.

Most of the students making the story = information conveyance articulation were male, and we went on to talk about the gendered nature of discourse, centering around Deborah Tannen's (1990) notions of "report talk" and "rapport talk," that the purpose of men's communication is to convey information in a hierarchical manner ("report talk"), whereas women are more often socialized to create community and reinforce shared perspectives in discourse ("rapport talk"). This was also done in the fall, but I did a much better job of explaining it in the spring, and students' engagement with the topic was more sophisticated. Also as in the fall, I discussed class and racial aspects of communication, such as the African American technique of call-and-response (Rose 1994); among other things I referenced Heath's (1983) study of the different racially significant ways in which two rural Piedmont Carolinas communities (particularly the children) acquire and use language. On the spring discussion in general, Anna notes that "many different students are contributing to this discussion. I can't even keep up with all of them. This class is a much better discussion class than the last" (FN, March 9).

Second, the implementation of the teacher as text was different in the spring than in the fall. In the fall I shared the story of my homophobic reaction to the suggestion by a male friend that we read a story together. When I related the story in the fall I used the word "fag," but substituted "gay" in the spring. Why? Two reasons: first, Lori's field notes were in mind. In lieu of devoting an entire period to exploring the nuances of the use of language—which in itself would most likely be lost on many, given the current stigma surrounding homosexuality—I decided to use a safer, more neutral term. Second, one individual in class was gay; that is, he was at least out to Jennifer and me, as he shared stories with us after one of the previous week's Kiva sessions. I did not want to put him in the position of feeling pressured to speak for his group in potentially hostile waters. That had been done to me in one of my graduate school classes and I vowed that I would never do that when I was as a professor, a conviction that I explicitly shared with each s101 class early in each semester.[4] I encouraged students to speak *from* their multisided experiences as members in social groups, but that they should not speak essentialistically *for* the groups.

That concern is very much in line with the third "EX" of the teacher as text project: explication of issues into larger theoretical frames of reference and understandings. I must show students how our personal perspectives are shaped by and shape larger social structures, but do so in such a way that empowers the student, rather than contributes to continued domination (e.g., pushing gay/lesbian students further into the closet). Sometimes even the attempt to highlight some structures was fraught with scalding tension; better to make foundational allusions and return to them at later dates than to try to explain everything in one shot.

This was the case at the conclusion of the spring storytelling day. When I asked the students to share their own stories, two male students responded with stories of drunken encounters with Others: "The in-class storytelling was pretty interesting. Of course they both happened to be drunken stories but we are at the university, I suppose. Walt mentioned doing more non-drunken stories on Wednesday . . . I think it's wise" (Jennifer FN, March 9). I did not get any more stories on Wednesday but began class with a reference to my wet white people as dogs stereotype story, which I shared to close out Monday's storytelling activities. As in the fall, I used that story to get students to think more about social stratification issues, and the power of oral communication to reinforce or contest inequality. I told the class to think about this recurring theme over spring break and beyond.

Overall, it's difficult to assign a label of success or failure to the storytelling days, as only a few students had previous experience with reading aloud. Indeed, for these few students storytelling is a rewarding, ongoing experience. Most of the other students in both fall and spring classes appeared to like the novelty of listening to stories in class, but did not write about the experience in the EC or in other communication with the assistants or me. In chapter 7 I will explore a pedagogical strategy that grew out of the storytelling days of the 1997–1998 autoethnography: "The Educational Storytelling Project" explicitly encourages students to engage the social dynamics of telling and listening to stories.

Deann—intervention "failed"

I believe that this is an accurate statement for the majority of the society. Some people feel that they are not affected by the media, but it's almost impossible to avoid any such impact. Examples of this statement are profoundly evident in our society by the clothes and shoes we wear, the restaurants we dine at, the movies we go see, the activities we are involved in, and many more.   —Week 1 image house posting

In the spring semester the students were required to post a message in the image house to let me know that their AltaVista EC accounts were working. I asked them to give me their thoughts on a "Calvin and Hobbes" cartoon in which Calvin (a six-year-old boy) tells his stuffed tiger Hobbes that he is immune to advertising pressures, and then bends down to inflate his $100 Reebok basketball shoes. Deann was the fourth student (of fifty-five total replies) to respond. I had high hopes that this senior would build on the insightful first posting throughout the semester, and would be an active voice in class. I was to be disappointed.

Consider her reactions to the *I Like It Like That* exercise that I described in chapter 3:

When the record producer tells the brothers he had a female assistant, I implied from their reaction that they automatically thought she was his secretary. This just enforces society's idea of female secretaries. Another interesting aspect was when one of the brothers reacted to the record producer saying the Bronx was around his neighborhood. He knew a white record producer wouldn't live in the Bronx. This is reaffirmed when the producer doesn't want to take her home. The Bronx has a certain connotation to people. (first viewing critical reactions)

When he told Lizette she wasn't what he wanted and then pointed to the other girl wearing a revealing outfit he wanted to entice the Mendez brothers with the physical looks of an assistant instead of a woman like Lizette who wanted to sell her ideas. (second viewing critical reactions)

This was different than the last time because I didn't see the woman the producer pointed to. (change in critical reactions)

The first reactions contain sociological insights we would expect after reading Deann's first-week image house posting. Her second viewing reactions are almost entirely descriptive, and the change in "critical" reactions is not critical at all. *All* of Deann's EC postings, media journal entries, and essays followed this pattern. That is, they were either entirely descriptive, or contained the general sociological concepts learned from other classes or the first few weeks of s101. For example, in a February 4 coffee house posting she only uses very basic concepts:

I definitely think the media coverage of the Clinton scandal overshadowed other news around the world. The Pope visiting Cuba and the crisis in Iraq should definitely be of great importance and should not be a side story to Clinton's alleged affair. This is characteristic of the media. The scandal provides a lot of gossip, hearsay, and shocking new discoveries that the people like to watch. Just like in advertising, the media tries to cover what they feel their audiences want to see. The majority of Americans probably know more about the Clinton scandal then they known about world affairs as in the Pope's visit to Cuba and the Iraq situation. I believe this is definitely a negative aspect of the media.

Deann was one of four or five students who never participated in class discussions, never e-mailed me or came to office hours, and did not attend the Kiva sessions that I will describe in the next two sections. In fact, she was so invisible that I did not know who she was until the last day of class when she turned in her final project early—I looked at the name and said to myself "So this is Deann!" Fortunately I usually only have one or two such students each semester; in the spring semester Deann was the one.

Deann, then, was a failed intervention in that the class seemed to have little effect on her life, other than as a class that had to be passed in order to graduate at the end of the semester. Perhaps "senioritis" was the reason she did not seem to spend much effort beyond minimal attention to the class and its objectives. Whatever the reason, she entered the class with a fairly sophisticated sociological imagination that was not changed by the class. So, it is minimally noteworthy that she was not *discouraged* from reading her social worlds somewhat critically. I hope that, at least, she continues this practice indefinitely.

Fall Kiva

I really enjoyed having the smaller group discussions instead of the regular class this week. I felt much more comfortable talking since the group was more intimate. Also, I became more acquainted with the people in the class. I think that having the groups meet in Kiva is also a very good idea because it's more cozy and informal, rather than sitting in desks in some classroom. I would definitely like to do this more in the future! (EC posting)

Even though reading a short story to students in a large college class is an unusual technique, it is still grounded in normal classroom procedures. The students did, after all, meet in the regular room, and I facilitated the discussion along preset thematic lines. bell hooks (2003:41), however, notes that "[t]eachers who have a vision of democratic education assume that learning is never confined solely to an institutionalized classroom." During the next week, I tried an even more radical move, getting students out of the usual routine altogether. As summarized by the EC message (posted immediately after experiencing the new technique), the students enjoyed the experiment and it helped them to synthesize issues and themes discussed during normal class. In the words of another student EC posting, "the group discussions were a hit."

What did I do, exactly? The following is a copy of the instructions posted to the EC on Monday, October 13:

One of the reasons that we have the EC is to give those who don't like speaking in large lecture halls a chance to be heard. Another method of encouraging expression is to have small group discussion. So instead of one big class on Wednesday we'll have several small classes in a more relaxed atmosphere: the "Garden Patch" in the Union's "Kiva" section. This is the area downstairs from the food court. Go to the end where the Pizza Hut stand is and look for the steps (you'll also see signs for the Garden Patch and the Kiva).

I'll conduct eight different mini-classes; you only have to go to ONE based on your last name in the following schedule:

Wednesday, October 15, 11:00–12:00: A-B
Wednesday, October 15, 12:00–1:00: C-D
Wednesday, October 15, 1:00–2:15: [See below]

Thursday, October 16, 11:00–12:00: E-Hol
Thursday, October 16, 12:00–1:00: Hor-L
Thursday, October 16, 1:00–2:00: M-Ri

Friday, October 17, 11:30–12:30: Ro-Ste
Friday, October 17, 12:30–1:30: Str-W

Now, I know that some of you will not be able to make your assigned times. In this case try to make one of the *other* sessions. If you can't make any of these, go to our normal meeting place (SB 150) on Wednesday at 1:00. In sum,

1. Try to make your assigned time.
2. Go to another session if you can't make your session.
3. Go to SB 150 as usual on Wednesday at the normal time if you can't do steps 1 or 2.

You should come prepared to talk about an issue or event you've been thinking about during the semester. The objective here is to discuss the thoughts of those whom we don't normally hear.

Note that students were supposed to have their own topics for discussion. In each session, however, students just had questions about course assignments when queried; I had to get the ball rolling. Once the ice was broken, the sessions ran smoothly and students shared a number of ideas and feelings. The most noteworthy observation is that students who did not normally speak in class were quite active here, as I had hoped and encouraged:

I think meeting in smaller groups was very useful and successful. I enjoyed getting to know some new classmates as well as getting to know some of the helpers. I'm not one to talk in class, so it was nice to be able to share my views with people. It also helped that we posed some of the same questions from the class. I think this exercise is extremely useful and would be good if we could do it again. Sometimes, it is easier to talk about sociological issues in a smaller group because you can focus on what each of you are saying and have a discussion. When you are in a large group, it becomes harder to get your point across. (EC posting)

I also enjoyed the group meetings we had last week, i'm not much of a talker but i do share some same views as other students. I really wish i could overcome the hatred i have of speaking in large groups. i think by having more of the small garden patch meetings i might get to know more people better and i'd feel more comfortable speaking in front of them. (EC posting)

Personally, I just wanted to let you know that I really enjoy when we have the opportunity to discuss our opinions, feelings, etc. with the students around us. It gives us the chance not only to meet other students, but to share our ideas. (e-mail)

Although the authors of these three responses did not become more active in the regular classroom discussions, a few others who participated in the Kiva sessions did. More important, though, in some form almost all students expressed themselves with others and attempted to engage sociological understandings. The extra time required to conduct the Kiva sessions was well worth the effort.

I conducted seven of the eight sessions. Attendance was heavy the first day (six in session 1, ten in session 2) and more sparse on Thursday and Friday (none for #4 and #7, one for #5, four for #6 and #8). Whether 4, 6, or 10 participants, all the students spoke and shared ideas—though, of course, in the larger sessions some students spoke more than others. The main goal of the Kiva sessions of encouraging voice was served. As for specific content of the discussion, topics were far-ranging, from questions about the course (including the role of the 494 crew) to debate about editorials in the campus newspaper. Again, however, the purpose of these sessions was to encourage shy students to begin to participate more actively as a starting point for increased critical literacy instead of looking at levels of critical literacy itself.

The 494 crew conducted the remaining session (the third overall), the meeting at the regular time and place. At first fifteen or so students were in attendance at that session, which dwindled to three after the crew repeated my instructions to try to attend one of the other sessions if possible. The session went smoothly after that:

really enjoyed and felt comfortable talking with the 3 students today . . . wish there would have been about 4 or 5 more . . . looking forward to next garden patch session . . . students seem more than satisfied with walt's teaching style . . . i could tell, they liked the more intimate setting, too. (Beeta FN, October 15)

was relieved that some students left, but disappointed that only three remained. felt kind of awkward at first considering there were as many people leading the discussion as there were students participating. the discussion turned out to be cool though. spent most of the time talking about the class itself: papers, electronic classroom, seating arrangements, class format, walt, etc. and all sorts of related tangents. the discussion seemed more like a group conversation, very relaxed, informal. everyone talked, very balanced. (Rob FN, October 15)

Walt comes in after class and asks how it went, etc. We offer highlights and during one point I observe that Beeta and Rob seemed very relaxed about the whole thing . . . not at all like it was their first time. Rob doesn't get my words of praise since there were only three students, but I jokingly tell him to hush up since my comment was directed more at Beeta anyway. I knew that Beeta was a bit nervous about what would be involved, but the truth is I think we all had a nice, even exchange of "control." All of us, including the three students. There really didn't seem to be a power imbalance. (Lori FN, October 15)

I had conducted similar Kiva sessions during previous years as the instructor of "race and ethnic relations" classes, and Lori had assisted me in the spring of 1997 (and even conducted two sessions entirely by herself), so she knew what to expect. Beeta and Rob were much more nervous about the experiment, since they had no experience with them (I did not do any sessions the semester Beeta took the class, and Rob was out of town during the week I held sessions for his class). Rob was able to attend the session I conducted just before their outing, so that helped him, but Beeta went in cold turkey. Before starting the discussion Lori told Beeta that everything would be fine in the discussion. She was annoyed that she had to do this, however:

I arrive late because I was on the other side of campus trying to get my academic career figured out. Beeta and Rob sitting off to the side. Beeta comes to me and says "thank God you're here." I reply something like "Oh, I knew it would be like this." I immediately feel regret because it's not Beeta or Rob's fault that I'm a little bitter. I've actually been a little resentful since Walt told me that I would be most in charge of Kiva sessions. I guess I just feel that he has higher expectations from me than other members of group. And while I've listened to him talk about having "different," not higher or lower expectations for us all, the end result is still that I end up doing more work. Also, last semester when I was on my own, it seemed like I was doing more than others are expected to do now. Maybe some of this goes back to my parents always applying more pressure to me than my brother, I don't know. I am certain that I didn't mean to snap at Beeta. She hasn't done anything wrong. (Lori FN, October 15)

Indeed, in this instance I did expect more from Lori, as she was more experienced in this particular task. In response to this field note and our discussion at the Friday afternoon group meeting, however, I made a conscious effort to even out the workload. Among other things, this resulted in Beeta and Rob conducting most of a second round of Kiva sessions that I decided to stage in week 10 of the semester. I'll discuss that in the "second helpings" section of this chapter. As always, I was extremely pleased that the 494 crew felt comfortable challenging my authority and procedures and that their comments had a positive effect on the class as a whole (in that I decided to conduct an extra round of the popular Kiva sessions to give the 494 crew more experience with leading discussions).

The decision to conduct extra sessions was also due to student requests in the EC:

I would like to say that I too enjoyed class on Wednesday. I don't talk in class and I think this was a good way to meet fellow class members and a great way to end the week. Just being able to sit back and talk about issues one on one was pretty cool. I don't think this should be done every week because then it would just get old. But I definitely think that we should do this a couple more times before the semester is over. I'm the type of person who likes to sit back and listen to what other people have to say and that's why I enjoy the large lectures that we have. But this was a lot of fun.

I really liked class Wednesday. It was a more comfortable setting. Plus, it let others feel more freely to speak their minds. We should do this again!

Two additional students posted messages that expressed the sentiment of the second posting. Although only half the class participated in the first round of Kiva sessions, they got a lot out of the experience. I looked forward to conducting a second round of sessions to meet their request for more, as well as to snare some of the students who missed the first round, thereby building on an already successful intervention. I also made plans to repeat the exercise in the spring.

Spring Kiva

Last week in the discussion I attended, Walt asked if sociology has answers for any of the problems it presents. I am interested to know what you guys think about that, because it really is a very complex question. I think that in understanding a problem lies the answer, but Walt added that a universal understanding of a problem, that is an understanding everyone accepts to be true, is pretty hard to come by. I was thinking about this further and I think Walt is right. Everyone creates their own reality and in that reality are our experiences and opinions. Since there are about 7 billion people on this planet (give or take a few billion) there are about 7 billion realities, so how can we meet in a common place and start to solve the problems within society? I don't know, any suggestions? (spring coffee house posting)

We can discern two immediate differences between the fall and spring reactions to the Kiva sessions. First, note that this posting doesn't say anything about how much the student enjoyed the session. Whereas there were eleven EC postings about the Kiva sessions in both semesters, all of the fall postings expressed gratitude for an alternative format and the opportunity to speak in a more intimate setting. Only two of the spring postings mentioned that, and, further, the reference was in passing and/or the introduction to the thesis of the posting. This leads to the second difference between the two classes: the spring class used the sessions as much more of a heuristic than the fall, using the debates of the sessions as a springboard for further reflection and refinement of their ideas in their own time. Their EC postings went beyond the fall class's preoccupation with coming to voice, and engaged each other on a number of substantive issues, such as the "generation X" debate:

I really enjoyed the Kiva discussion groups. I think it is a great way to bring up issues we may not have time to discuss in class. The topic that interested me the most was Gen X. I am very proud to be a member of our generation. It is sad that we have been given the term Generation X implying we have no ambitions or future. I think most people in our generation know for a fact this is not true. We are the technological link to the future. We participate in many charity organizations and are interested in politics and community. There are so many groups sponsored by people of our generation that do so much good for society. If we were not around, those groups would not exist. We will continue the positive things the baby boomers accomplished, and fix the problems they caused. What it comes down to is—every previous generation has been given a bad name by their parents' generation. Every generation thinks the following generation is lazy and not as positive as their own generation. This is a historical trend that hopefully our generation can stop. Having a positive outlook for the future means having faith in ourselves and in our children. We know we are a great generation, and we can trust the next generation can be even better. (EC posting)

I agree with everything that was said about our generation being more technological and this sort of progress will continue to grow throughout the different generations but I'm a bit concerned at how much this will progress. If we keep creating more and more gadgets won't our society eventually wind up jobless and lazy? I mean it's to the point now where we don't have to walk anywhere not even to change a television station let alone to get to work or school. Plus I'm a little concerned about the job market in a few years. I worry because what if there's no need for human labor. What if the only jobs available are building robots to do all the other jobs? This sort of progression is what scares me. (EC posting)

Overall, the oft-seen (and discussed in previous chapters) differential inflection of critical literacy emerged, as the fall class learned a new avenue of expression, while the spring class used the experience to extend and refine previous thoughts and perceptions. As discussed throughout the book, however, both dynamics are important and well suited for each class, given its demographics. Also, of course, both dynamics were present in both courses, even though one form was more in evidence than the other. Indeed, these components are normal components of many classrooms, Pensieves or not. The objective of a classroom as Pensieve, however, is to try to encourage even more contemplation of thoughts and perceptions (about internal and external class subjects) within a framework in which students continually make contingent, open-ended articulations: students never get "the" Truth, but make pragmatic truths. The Kiva sessions provided an opportunity to advance this project.

The setup for the spring session was slightly different from the fall, as the spring class did not meet until 2:30 (when the Kiva closed), compared to the 1:00 start in the fall. So I conducted a session in my office at the regular time on Wednesday, March 4, but encouraged the students to attend one of the eight one-hour sessions at the Kiva if at all possible. These were held at 11:30–12:30, 12:30–1:30, and 1:30–2:30 on Wednesday and Thursday, and at 11:30–12:30 and 12:30–1:30 on Friday.

In contrast to the fall pattern of heavy attendance of first few sessions and sparse turnout for later sessions, spring attendance was relatively even: 1, 6, 15, 8, 4, 7, 3, and 8 students. I also had two students attend the

Wednesday 2:30 session in my office. With the exception of the third session (with fifteen students) all the students talked, including those who did not normally do so in class. As in the fall, the spring Kiva sessions helped many to continue efforts to come to voice.

The fifteen-person outing was a bit too large, and two or three students just listened for most of the entire period. Initially, however, it was worse, as eighteen students showed up. Only three left after I encouraged those who could make another session to leave and attend one of those. I suppose that I should have tried harder, as (1) some students were not able to speak much, as previously mentioned, and (2) I was yelled at by the manager the next day for taking up too much space. Well, perhaps "yell" is not the right word, as he maintained soft tones throughout our discussion and was well within his rights to say that my students—who were not eating anything, though a few purchased drinks—took up space that could have been used by paying customers; they had, in fact, received a few complaints. He added that he would be happy to make arrangements to have the space be available for after-hours use. I told him no thanks, and the hassle (small that it was) was one of the reasons why I decided not to hold a second round of Kiva sessions, as I will elaborate at the end of the chapter.

The large size of the third session did not dampen the quality of conversation, however. As was the case in all the other sessions, discussion was far-ranging and covered complicated topics, such as that expressed in the second of the previous EC postings, by a participant of the large session. The large session also included an interesting illustration of the effects of the teacher as text: one student ("Phil" of chapter 3's second spotlight box) told me that he wouldn't normally admit this to his instructors, but he proudly wore the label of a "Slacker" who believed in doing as little work as possible. In an e-mail he said that he confided this since he believed that I wouldn't hold it against him. In fact, when he later went beyond normal assignment requirements (by doing his media journal as a web page) I asked about the apparent contradiction. He responded that for him it actually entailed less work to collect and organize materials on the web, and that "I'm not going to say you gave me a better grade because my journal looked pretty, you're the last instructor I would expect that from" (post-semester e-mail). As I noted in Phil's spotlight box, however, this e-mail came after the semester grades were submitted; Phil didn't want to take any chances that he could be wrong about a possible reprisal!

Additionally, spring students felt free to include my Kiva statements and questions into their EC postings, such as in this section's epigraph, and the following posting:

I think the Kiva small group discussions were very interesting and informative. The talk about Puff Daddy and how the white and African American groups respond to his music was very interesting. I think the [black] community feels that he is taking "their" music and making it something it "shouldn't be." Walt made the point that some African Americans feel that Puff is making hip hop music "impure" by adding a traditionally white brand of music. The impact that Puff and his music have had on this generation is quite astounding, whether you think what he does is "music" or not.

Once again, the spring class was operating in a mode of critical literacy where they reframed and extended their own perspectives: rather than simply talking about new knowledges gained, they juxtaposed fragments from their own previous experiences with elements from other sources (me, other students, readings, etc), as did the student of this posting.

The students also used Jennifer and her perspectives in that effort. Jennifer attended two sessions on Thursday and was the co-facilitator of the last session on Friday:

On Friday Walt wanted me to lead the discussion. We did more of a tag-team, though I did receive primary responsibility. . . . We brought in gender to spice things up a bit, using "Delia" [a mail-order catalog] as reference. Speaking of spice, the Spice Girls came up as well. I enjoyed the feedback from all the members of this discussion [although] I sensed the 2 sorority girls disliked my feminist take on a few issues. (Jennifer FN, March 6)

Even the two self-identified sorority sisters, however, were vocal and tried to look at topics (such as the sexual politics of the TV show *Dawson's Creek*) sociologically. I was pleased by the effort of this group, as I was by that exerted in all the sessions of the spring. By this week—the eighth of the fifteen-week semester—students were active and engaged and eager to learn. I was looking forward to the second half of the semester, and hoped that it would continue in the same vein, which it did.

Doug—"successful" intervention

Just wanted to send out a little feedback. Well, I'm sure this is true for many people in the class. This was my first class at IU that did not have any tests. I was a little bit skeptical about this at first. It seemed like I would be able to just cruise through without really learning anything. After the first paper, I actually realized that I was learning things. Instead of having to just memorize data to write down on a scantron, I actually had some knowledge of class material that I could use. As the semester went on I started learning much more. I was really surprised at how much I did learn by the end of the semester. Now, I am one of those people who can't watch anything without being critical anymore. It feels like I really used what we learned in this class more than any other class I have had. I know I'll remember this stuff long term, and not just short term for a test.

—EC POSTING ("Feedback" folder)

As articulated in this posting from the last week of the fall class, Doug got a lot out of the course. He specifically mentions his new appreciation for the value of a non test-based course, which may be especially significant given that Doug was a computer science major: this is a case in which someone trained in "hard" science methodologies has embraced some of the "soft" social science techniques of inquiry. Doug is a successful intervention in that he had vocal skepticism about the critical literacy project but, in the end, thinks that he has gained a valuable experience.

In the feedback posting Doug says that "I am one of those people who can't watch anything without being critical anymore." Let's look at the progression of his analytical abilities:

It seemed true that he would not want to take his car to the Bronx, but why would he go alone. It is too dangerous to do that. Price didn't know what the guys thought was attractive. He only knew what he thought they liked. (reactions to first viewing of *I Like It Like That* clip; see chapter 3 for description)

It seems as if the restaurant that they are at is somewhat shabby for a record company to sign a big client. Was the Ferrari parked in the back alley? Gender wise, Price definitely expected a good looking woman to walk in the door. He is so rich and powerful that he probably does not have to deal with ugly women often. (second viewing critical reactions)

This is a much different viewpoint from what I had last time. I don't believe I noticed anything sociologically last time. I was more interested in the production aspect. I didn't even notice that he got a latino girl to talk to latino clients. I just let that cruise by last time. (change in critical reactions, first to second viewings)

During the first scene, Price does not have faith in Lisette, but when she tells him about the group on the tape, it seems like that is a turning point where he comes to believe in her. (third viewing critical reactions)

I really didn't notice these things last time. I thought he just offered her a job because he felt sorry for her, but now it seems like he needs her. (change in critical reactions, second to third viewings)

As we can see, Doug mainly went from making no sociological connections to creating general observations about inequality. Note, though, that Doug is one of the very few students (less than ten of over 120 total over the year) to list his socioeconomic status as "upper class," so while it would be nice to see the development of more sophisticated analysis, it may be significant that previously invisible dynamics (in his case; see below) are being noticed. Even more encouragingly, he is sharing his discoveries with others: in his media journal he notes that he is surprised that pointing out sociological aspects of media representations to his friends does not ruin the experience. He also brought a family member to class on two occasions. I usually have two or three student bring a friend to one class to check out my methods, but twice is a (very nice) first!

Doug was one of the most vocal members in the fall class, in both the physical classroom and the EC. In response to a week 4 debate house question about the value of using videoclips in class, he writes:

You may or may not agree with what is said after the clips are shown, but still, they produce feedback from the classroom. If the class reacts in all these different ways such as you feeling nothing, me feeling amused, and other people feeling different things about the prodigy video, than that finally is an accurate portrayal of Society, which this class is trying to study. In society, everyone will not agree, and your answer to this debate question, and my answer are perfect examples of this. That's what makes our society great. I would die if I didn't have anyone to debate with. I love debating, and try to do as much as I can in class. The videos just stimulate my thinking.

From day one Doug was willing to debate any and all positions, but as the semester progressed his ideas became more sociologically grounded, and his sociological imagination blossomed, such as in his comments about *Space Traders:*

I was surprised Doug said what he did. I didn't expect him to admit Reaganomics exploited urban blacks. He didn't really say it, but he acknowledged it. What does this mean? (Rob FN, October 27)

What it means is that Doug has taken a few steps into the matrix of domination, here thinking about class privilege, to which he was frequently oblivious in his in-class comments. For instance, during a mid-semester class there were audible moans and rolled eyes from his fellow students when he insisted that everyone can afford a home computer with Internet access if they were willing to make sacrifices. Recall that Collins (1991) says that it is very difficult for us to investigate our social advantages, especially in conjunction with our disadvantages. By the end of the semester Doug was starting to qualify his statements, realizing that his position and experience are not universal (e.g., he later said that it's easier and necessary for those in high-paying information-dependent industries like computer science to maintain home computer stations, but soon everyone would have few problems). While his acknowledgment of class privilege was still somewhat rudimentary at the end of the semester, he *was* starting to enter the matrix. Moreover, this path appears to be one he'll continue in the future. In Doug's case, then, the critical intervention has been a success.

Second Helpings

Altogether, fifty-four of the sixty-six members of the spring class attended one of the spring Kiva sessions. Since the vast majority of students participated in this breaking of the normal class frame, I decided that I did not need to conduct a second round of sessions. Also, as noted earlier, since I was taken to task by the manager of the Kiva for taking up space I was disinclined to return.

The fall class, however, needed a second round of sessions, for two reasons. First, less than half (twenty-eight of sixty-five) of the students attended the first round, so most of the students had not experienced this particular strategy. Second, the strategy itself needed to be more fully engaged. As previously noted, the fall students who did attend the sessions primarily used it to come to voice, in the sense of expressing themselves openly. bell hooks (1994a:148), however, notes that "coming to voice is not just the act of telling one's experience. It is using that telling strategically—to come to voice so that you can also speak freely about other subjects." Amy Lee (2000:142) adds, "voice signifies discourse as a means to and product of power, recognizing that the means by which a subject claims discursive power is intimately linked to the position envisioned for her by the discourse itself." I wanted the students to use their voice as a heuristic, to learn to make connections with other perspectives and issues as these presented themselves in social interaction.

In the fall, therefore, I organized a second round of discussion hours at the Kiva on November 5–7 (week 10 of the semester). As with the first round, we conducted seven sessions in the Kiva and one session in the normal classroom. As was also the case with the first round, attendance was heavy on day one, and tailed off later in the week (Wednesday: #1 = 8, #2 = 11, #3 = 4 [session at regular time and place; attend if can't do any other]; Thursday: #4 = 1, #5 = 3, #6 = 2; Friday: #7 = 3, #8 = 2). Of these thirty-four students, twenty did not attend the first round of sessions. In sum, fifty-eight of sixty-five students attended at least one fall Kiva session.

The sessions were primarily conducted by the 494 crew the second time around. Beeta led discussion sessions 3 (in the normal class room at the regular class time) and 5; Lori led session number 6; and Rob led sessions 1, 2, 7, and 8. I sat in on the very last session with Rob, and Beeta sat in on Lori's session. Note that Lori only conducted one session, while Beeta attended three, and Rob led four. I did this to even out the workload among the crew, as discussed earlier.

I also wanted the crew to lead the sessions in an effort to gauge how students would respond to assistant-led discussions instead of when I was the facilitator. Unfortunately, I cannot draw many conclusions about this question because Lori and Beeta's sessions were small, and they both spent the vast majority of their time discussing my instructions for the upcoming second essay. In each session the students criticized my occasional use of jargon, especially in the instructions for essay 2. So, it is useful to know that students were comfortable (on at least a basic level) expressing discontent, to each other, the assistants, and me (as discussed in earlier chapters). A major component of creating the classroom as Pensieve is the willingness to criticize any component of that space, and to make adjustments in progress; in response I simplified language in instructions for the final project and reduced the number of $5.00 words in lectures.

Rob's sessions, however, were different. On Wednesday eight students attended his first session, and eleven were in the second. During the previous week we had discussed *Space Traders* (see chapter 4) so Rob made that a main topic of conversation:

somehow, we talked about space traders for 20–30 minutes. nothing extraordinary. one student commented that minorities make up 25% of the population and if hypothetically they all voted against the trade, you would only need 25% of the white vote to reach 50%. we entertain this "new way to look at it" for a while. (Rob FN, November 5 re: first session)

overall second session was very similar to the first one (in terms of context), but was more fluid in conversation. started off the same way. asked who thought the trade would pass, three or four students said it would, including [two students], don't remember others. rest said it wouldn't pass. asked why they felt the way they did. nobody had much to say except [same two students]. (Rob FN, November 5 re: second session)

As noted, however, the students were not very engaged. This can most likely be attributed to (1) student fatigue with a topic that was extensively discussed for the past two weeks, and, even more significantly, the (2) teacher as text: Rob is Mexican American and throughout the course constructed a "militant" persona. As explored in chapter 4, Rob thought that the hard and unpleasant facts of the contemporary United States should be repeatedly introduced and emphasized, rather than my more subtle approach.

That was illustrated in Rob's last session, the one I sat in on:

> started talking about space traders, walt remained quiet. both girls believed the trade would not pass. i brought up the routine, one out of every two black children [live in poverty]. ["Pam"] quickly responded with a "what does that have to do with anything" sort of comment. she continued and said that she would not use that stat to prove the trade would pass. she did this in a sort of condescending, matter-of-fact manner. i agreed with her, and said i was not trying to prove the trade would pass, but rather i was merely trying to demonstrate the present state of marginality for blacks in this country—which is something that should be considered before one concludes the trade would fail. of course, Pam didn't understand this (how convenient it would be to choose what you wish NOT to understand—how convenient it would be to have no soul), so i tried to further augment [my line of thought], but i was stepping all over my words. fortunate for me, walt decided this would be a good time to break his code of silence, and he articulated my point. walt went off for a while and took the issue much deeper than i could have. Pam nodded her head in understanding, but her eyes said she was not bothering herself to understand. (Rob FN, November 7)

I shared Rob's sense that my discussion of *Space Traders* was falling on deaf ears, so I decided to switch tactics, and returned to the discussion of the fraternity that was suspended just before *Space Traders* week. Both of the women at the discussion were in sororities, and made arguments that although racism may exist in the Greek system, their two houses were not racist. They also disagreed with my suggestion that sororities may discriminate by class, ethnicity, or physical beauty. Rob notes that "this was a very intense, polarized discussion. Intense does not mean heated, the discussion never escaped the realm of civility. Polarized means there were two distinct, opposite sides" (FN, November 7).

I went on to introduce the matrix of domination theory into the debate, which Rob discusses in a November 7 field note:

> eventually walt tried to explain how the matrix of domination may be influencing their views, how it may be outside their interest to recognize the negatives of the greek system. they were not easily convinced, however, toward the end of the discussion, walt trapped them (so to speak) into acknowledging, if not recognizing, a clear example of this. i don't recall the specifics, although i wish i did (perhaps walt does), but walt basically asked the girls to generalize and estimate a percentage of the greek members that would advocate a certain view, position,

belief, something—i don't know—it may have been related to space traders. regardless the question was related to a critical issue, and both girls said they could not speak for the entire greek system. "Pam" said: "i don't know what everybody would say." recognizing walt's ploy, i responded: "of course you don't know everybody's (greek members) opinion, you wouldn't know unless you performed a survey, i don't think walt expected you to have conducted a survey, so why don't you just speculate?" both girls refused or were not able to speculate. walt told them that their inability to speculate was an example of the matrix. it was not in their best interest to give a response, so they did not. both girls looked confused, but on this occasion, confusion meant understanding.

My question had been: "Would most sorority members say they don't consider attractiveness when making membership considerations?" After much back and forth about their struggle in the matrix of domination, Pam asked, "What can I do to improve the situation at my house?" to which "Eliza" nodded. This is the same Eliza of the previous chapter, who went on to end her *Space Traders* essay with "In conclusion, I really enjoyed this part of our class. I thought it was a very unique kind of paper that made you really think about how people in today's society can be." I believe that the Kiva session was part of that comment. In her final media journal entry, Pam stated that she's become much more of a critical thinker in general because of the class. I hope that this includes institutions and practices in which she's heavily invested. In general, the second round of Kiva sessions helped the participating students learn that their specific articulations were due to the place in which they were made and to the participants involved.[5]

In the fall I also conducted a second "storytelling day," on Monday, November 24. I must admit that I did this as much out of a need for a break in routine as for theoretical reasons (obtaining more data on frame-breaking activities). This was the session just before Thanksgiving break, and I was feeling the effects of the past twelve weeks of intense classes. So instead of coming up with new lecture material, I figured it would be easier to repeat previous strategy, with a new twist: asked each member of the 494 crew to bring in a story to read. Alas, Beeta was absent due to illness, and Lori forgot to bring in a story, and the selection that I asked her to randomly pick out of the book *Einstein's Dreams* (Lightman 1993)—a collection of meditations on alternate worlds with different laws of time and space—was a boring, stream-of-consciousness description of memories past. Stories read by Rob and I also did not generate much enthusiasm, as both were too dense (mine from *Einstein's Dreams;* Rob's a fable on the origin of rationality) for the lethargic class: less than half bothered to show up, and most of them looked like they were ready to go ten minutes after they walked in. I dismissed class early, hoping that would contribute to a fresh start when classes resumed.

Before closing this chapter I will mention a final frame-breaking (from the normal classroom setup) activity conducted in both semesters: informal discussions of new theatrical movies at a local off-campus restaurant. In the fall I asked those who were interested in discussing the then-current movie *In and Out* (about a gay male high school teacher being outed by a former student just before the teacher's heterosexual wedding) to meet Lori and me at The Encore Cafe, a jazz music-filled space converted from a garage that is more popular with graduate students and professors than undergraduates. I stressed that this was not a required event, and that it would not affect their grades in any way. On Sunday, October 26, Jennifer brought a friend who was visiting from another state university to the meeting. The four of us had a conversation for about an hour, ranging from textual analysis of the movie (e.g., were the characters stereotypes?), to class theories (such as the matrix of domination: why did the movie represent women disturbingly while trying to celebrate homosexuality?), to comments about the Academy (public universities in general and Indiana University in particular). Although I wished that more people could have attended, the small group did have its advantage in a congenial level of comfort from the beginning.

In the spring the movie of discussion was *Wag the Dog*, about presidential advisors creating a fake war to divert media attention from a sex scandal. As in the fall, I choose this movie out a combination of personal interest, relevance to current class topics, and comments by students on the movie. Four students had posted coffee house messages about their enjoyment of *Wag the Dog*, and one student wrote that she looked forward to seeing it. None of these five, however, attended the Sunday, February 1, discussion at The Encore Cafe. Jennifer led the discussion, and two students attended to round out our foursome. As in the fall, the discussion was wide-ranging in scope, and both students said they enjoyed the discussion and learned a lot. One student was a freshman and stated that she was a little nervous about talking to instructors, but after that she talked with me before each assignment to make sure she was on the right track. The other student was a junior and excelled in class throughout without much direction from me above and beyond general instructions.

Overall, frame-breaking activities like storytelling days, Kiva sessions, and informal movie discussions provided alternative means of expression for the students and assisted them in the overall goal of creating the classroom as Pensieve. The results of these activities suggest that Pensieves are place-dependent: students make different articulations in different physical locations and configurations. Breaking taken-for-granted frames of instruction assists instructors in our quest to "engage students in revisioning the concepts by which they organize their lives as well as to rethink . . . lived, material relations" (Lee 2000:150). In the college classroom as Pensieve the participants continually sketch and resketch contextual frameworks in order to learn and live media culture to create more flexible identities, empower themselves and Others, and explore alternative social worlds.

Chapter Six

Conjuring the Future

To be haunted and to write from that location, to take on the condition of what you study, is not a methodology or a consciousness you can simply adopt or adapt as a set of rules or an identity; it produces its own insights and blindnesses. [It] is about making a contact that changes you and refashions the social relations in which you are located. It is about putting life back in where only a vague memory or bare trace was visible to those who bothered to look. . . . Sociology . . . has an extraordinary mandate . . . to conjure up social life. Conjuring is a particular form of calling up and calling out the forces that make things what they are in order to fix a troubling situation. As a mode of apprehension and reformation, conjuring merges the analytical, the procedural, the imaginative, and the effervescent. —AVERY GORDON, *Ghostly Matters*

In Pensieves the instructors want to make lasting impressions on their students. We "conjure," entering often uncomfortable situations in order to continually make and remake understandings of the social from memories of the past, perceptions of the present, and anticipations of the future. Gordon writes that when we attempt to conjure social reality, we are changed on a variety of levels, merging methodological, theoretical, and conceptual interests into an activist agenda of creating more democratic and empowering spaces. We become "haunted" in the process of continually questioning our places in the world: we juxtapose real and imagined social conditions to make contingent articulations on who we were, are, and should be, but these articulations are never fully sedimented. Our understandings of our social worlds are—and should be—in constant motion. We speak lower frequencies that are tough to hear and process.

Although not calling it such, I have been investigating the haunting of myself, my assistants, and my students throughout the 1997–1998 autoethnography. As we have seen, on many occasions the classes of that project were forced to deal with issues and events that we would rather not, and we deployed a number of tools to try to make sense of our reluctance, to transform it into an empowering experience. In this chapter I will examine some of the experiences of my undergraduate assistants in this effort. I will also explore the results of an extension of the 1997–1998 autoethnography, in which twelve students met in weekly 1998–1999 discussions of the TV show *The X-Files*. I not only wanted all involved in the autoethnography to conjure the "media and society" class as Pensieve, I wanted to create tools with which we can apply experiences created there to the conjuring of other spaces as well. Ideally, students will not only use skills generated in the classroom in the year after the formal class ends, they will use the experience as a foundation for continual, never-ending evolution.

"The Unknown Student"—intervention "failed"

As decreed by the Indiana University Institutional Review Board, I disseminated informed consent statements at the end of each semester, and did not view them until after grades were posted.[1] The informed consent statements gave me permission to use data from in-class observations and analysis of course assignments in research publications. Fifty of sixty-five students returned signed forms in the fall, and fifty-four of sixty-six students returned signed forms in the spring. The informed consent statements were passed out with the course evaluations, and the return rate of the informed consent statement roughly paralleled completion of the evaluations: fifty-five students completed evaluations in the fall, and fifty-two completed them in the spring. Note, however, that not all students received the forms, as some students were absent on evaluation days.

So, at first we may be tempted to conclude that all but five of those receiving forms in the fall choose to grant informed consent while completing evaluations, but how, then, would we explain the two spring students who gave consent but did not complete the evaluations; shouldn't it be the other way around (complete evaluation, do not grant consent, or don't complete either)? The main point, however, is that the great majority of students *did* grant informed consent. In that sense, the overall attempt of creating a Pensieve and making a basic intervention was, at the very least, tolerated.

But what about those students who deliberately withheld informed consent? Why did some not want data about them to be used? We will never know the myriad reasons, but it is important to note here that the denials were not systematic in terms of social locations (e.g., all white men). Leaving out (of course) specifics, those who did not sign the informed consent statements were men and women, white and of color, young and old (chronologically and by class standing), College of Arts and Sciences (COAS) majors and non-COAS majors. Indeed, a vast spectrum of identities was represented in those who did not sign the informed consent statements as well as in those who did.

I consider "the unknown student"—the student who did not sign the informed consent statement—a failed intervention because I wanted everyone to feel empowered by my class. Of course, this is an unrealistic expectation, in any class, be it Pensieve or not. My efforts to maximize student empowerment, however, will never end.

An Extracurricular Pensieve

Recently, I have been thinking about political subjects who imagine their position in the world and act, but who are also subject to state power. I have been thinking about the way the state manifests its power, especially when it does not call attention to its presence. —WAHNEEMA LUBIANO, "Like Being Mugged by a Metaphor"

As we have seen throughout the book, it can be difficult to help college students enter the Pensieve and construct themselves as subjects who (following Lubiano in the epigraph) speak the lower frequencies and call power (of the State as well as other institutions) into hearable range. Strange texts such as the movie *Space Traders* and the TV show *The X-Files* are useful in helping college students see themselves as actors who should constantly reimagine their social positions and act to create new social contexts and meanings.

The 1998–1999 autoethnography was conducted during the fifth season of *The X-Files*, which most believed was still great.[2] Among other things, we witnessed investigations of a sentient computer program in "Kill Switch," militias in "The Pine Bluff Variant," and small-town Americana in "The Post-Modern Prometheus." I'm sure that the students in my Monday classes of the 1997–1998 academic year dreaded the inevitable "Did anyone catch last night's *X-Files*?" question, and the spring semester students were absolutely thrilled when we watched and discussed "The Post-Modern Prometheus" in its entirety, as discussed in chapter 4. What else, though, is a sci-fi geek gonna do with a favorite show that's not only entertaining, but also creates learning opportunities?

Here's one thing: start a focus group of interested students who would watch *The X-Files* every week and then gather as group to discuss it. During the 1998–1999 season (year 6 of the show) I did this, with twelve former autoethnography students participating in two groups of six students each. The point? Yes, pure entertainment was one objective, but I also wanted to extend discussion started in the autoethnography on the following question: can a televisual work of fiction continue students' investigation of powerful real-life understandings learned in the Pensieve? I believe that it can, and did in our "salon" meetings, where we discussed all sorts of social issues and events. Discussing elements of the show triggered memories and experiences from real life, which can lead to powerful new understandings on multiple levels.

The twelve students were from the both semesters of the autoethnography, responding to the following e-mail sent out to all in the summer of 1998:

In the spring s101 "media and society" course the class analyzed an episode of the TV show *The X-Files*, which was used as part of a research project on students' use of electronic media. In an extension of the research project, former s101 students will watch and discuss episodes of *The X-Files* in the 1998–1999 TV season. There are four ways to participate. You can choose several of the following options, or choose only one: (1) send me e-mail whenever you have observations you wish to share; (2) periodically post messages in an AltaVista forum; (3) keep a media journal about your experiences, as you did in s101; or (4) meet in a weekly focus group with me, Jennifer Richie (the T.A. in the spring), and a small group of other students, which will be ethnographically observed. Students who choose options (3) and (4) will be eligible to receive 1 hour of course credit (sociology s495, "Individual Readings and Research") in the Spring 1999 semester. You can devote as much or as little time to this project as you want, but generally—in addition to watching the 1 hour show—options (1) and (2) take 30 minutes, and options (3) and (4) take 1 hour.

Twenty-two former students signed up for the extension, of which fifteen wanted to participate in the focus groups, which met after each new episode in the November 1998-May 1999 TV season (there were twenty-two episodes in all). The participants consisted of students from a wide range of academic abilities (A, B, and C students) in general and as demonstrated in "media and society." The group also contained a mixture of those participating because they loved the show and some who just wanted an easy course credit. Two of the twelve who stayed with the focus group over the entire year explicitly said that they liked me and my overall research agenda, and wanted to further its objectives. All, however, made interesting comments throughout the year and learned new things about themselves and their social worlds.

Many 100-level introductory social science classes in large public universities are mob settings, with 100, 200, even 300+ students enrolled. In the autoethnography I had enrollments of sixty-five and sixty-six, but even such relatively intimate contexts make it tough to get good sustained discussion going. Even when the instructor uses a text—like a contemporary television show—that students enjoy, there's never enough time to have more than a handful of students participate, and then only two or three viewpoints are expressed, and these usually don't completely explore the hidden aspects of institutional structures. Furthermore, generating more than one viewpoint assumes that the instructor selected texts of real interest; in other chapters I discussed how some students did not raise much above saying "it was interesting."

Here's where a science fiction TV show like *The X-Files* can come in. While only a minority of students will admit to being fans, the majority has had some exposure to the genre, and knows its conventions. An instructor can use sci-fi TV in the class to stimulate interest and discussion of current events. Specifically, most students will regard sci-fi as "strange" and "unreal"; instructors can employ this opinion to make connections to strange aspects of real life that most see but do not want to investigate. With its history of utopian possibility, teachers can use sci-fi TV to help students question taken-for-granted assumptions and form alternative possibilities that work against ever-expanding social stratification and inequality. In *The X-Files,* for instance, "its narrative does more than teach us to distrust authority; it teaches us to trust ourselves. If we can not rely on blind faith in government or science, we must rely on our own abilities to judge external truths and discover internal truths" (Bellon 1999:152). "*The X-Files* deploys a mode of popular paranoia to subvert received attitudes, beliefs, and ways of seeing common to popular television" (Kellner 1999:169).

Participation in a sci-fi salon continues the critique begun in the classroom as Pensieve. Actually, it extends and depends the process, as students can more fully explore topics and concerns given that they have more time and are in a relaxed atmosphere (e.g., there's no pressure of grades). In my *X-Files* salon the students and I met in each week that a new episode aired, in an off-campus restaurant that—along with lots of informal off-topic discussion in each meeting—created a casual and friendly environment. We had quite a bit of fun discussing the minutiae of each episode. Note, however, that the objective was not to create close textual analysis of each episode, it was to use elements from the show to investigate a wide range of social experiences and understandings. "Because it is unwilling to bow to the authority of accepted science—because it is about the search for the nature of reality—[*The X-Files*] can open our eyes to what is happening around us here and now" (Bellon 1999:152).

Let's examine the reaction to one particular episode as an example. First, a brief thumbnail description of "Arcadia" (Carter 1999) from the episode guide on the official site (www.thexfiles.com):

Welcome to "The Falls at Arcadia," one of the nation's top-rated planned communities. Unfortunately, three couples have vanished from the neighborhood over the past seven years. Mulder and Scully go undercover and pose as new home buyers to investigate the strange disappearances.

Helpful resident Big Mike, a veterinarian, and next-door neighbors, Win and Cami Schroeder, help Mulder and Scully get squared away on move-in day. However, Win balks when Mulder wants to erect a portable basketball hoop; this definitely goes against the community's strict regulations. Win suggests that Mulder take up the issue with Homeowner president, Gene Gogolak.

When Big Mike suddenly disappears, the Shroeders simply explain to Mulder and Scully that he went away on business. Scully and Mulder pay a visit to Gogolak, who tells them that regulations forbid the basketball hoop in the front driveway. He explains that rules are rules, and though it may seem tough to get used to, theirs is a system that works. Mulder then changes the subject to Gogolak's decor. Gogolak explains that most of his antiques are Nepalese and Tibetan; he owns Pier 9 Imports and travels to the Far East often for business.

The Shroeders invite Mulder and Scully to dinner and Mulder presses the issue of Big Mike's disappearance. When Cami becomes uncomfortable with the topic and excuses herself to take the dog out, Scully accompanies her. During their walk, the dog gets loose and scrambles into a nearby storm drain. As Scully tries to fish out the lost pooch, she finds a caduceus necklace worn by Big Mike covered in what appears to be blood.

Scully has the "blood" analyzed, only to find that it is basically garbage; the neighborhood was built atop an old landfill. Mulder theorizes that the Klines are buried in the yard somewhere, and while digging a hole to find them, he dredges up a Malaysian artifact with a sticker showing that it came from Pier 9 Imports. Mulder confronts Gogolak with the theory that Gogolak, while on the trips to Far East, learned of the tulpa, or Tibetan thought-form, a creature willed into existence by one who possesses the ability. He believes Gogolak created this creature formed by garbage to keep the residents in check.

Meantime, back at home, Scully is surprised by Big Mike who is alive but mauled. He reveals that he was attacked by the creature, but managed to escape. He tells Scully that the creature is coming for her because her "husband" has broken the rules. Big Mike barricades Scully in the closet and fights off the approaching monster. The firing gunshots warn Mulder, who races home, with

Gogolak in tow. Mulder stops to handcuff Gogolak to the mailbox before going inside to help Scully. Outside, Gogolak is attacked by his own creation. With his death, the tulpa dies as well, disintegrating at Mulder's feet.

Although the usual subjects arose in our discussion of this episode—gender politics, racial inclusions and exclusions, concerns about technology—the students were particularly keen to discuss the politics of gated and planned communities. Some expressed shock and disbelief that communities exist that regulate the color of your house, the use of patio furniture, the length of the grass, and so on, but others assured them that this is indeed the case, and they collectively explored the good, the bad, and the ugly about this state of affairs:

Overall had a good discussion about gated and planned communities, and online privacy. No one wants to live in a gated community. (Walt FN, March 8)

As for the "perfect neighborhood," I haven't seen one. Do they really exist? (journal entry)

So, the overall message was totally awesome, and it can be applied to more than just gated communities (i.e., sororities, fraternities, etc.). Being like everyone else is so dangerous. (journal entry)

I do not understand people that try so hard to be just like everyone else, to the point of losing their own identity. And, I don't understand people that are so accepting of ridiculous rules. Do they need these things to have control of their lives? (journal entry)

The show does tap on some cultural issues that need to be noticed. Our society is growing inward and communities are building high fences. (journal entry)

I'm reminded of the rich towns of California that are closed to the public, or even worse, Disney World, where the Constitution does not apply. Individual rights are not recognized when eight-year-olds that allegedly steal Mickey Mouse ears get strip-searched. There is no denying that our melting pot more resembles a corporate rock. (journal entry)

I attempted to describe Celebration, USA [a planned community built by the Disney corporation; see Ross 1999] to my roommate, though I doubt I did it justice. (journal entry)

It was interesting to see the show make fun of how crazy subdivisions can get with rules: to make everyone "fit in" and have aesthetically pleasing plots/homes. (journal entry)

All I could think of was *The Stepford Wives,* [a movie] where everyone was the same. I also thought of Machiavelli, who wrote of rule with fear to control the people. (journal entry)

The stereotypes run rampant in this episode. (journal entry)

I found it somewhat funny because my parents are moving [from] an older neighborhood where each house is unique and different [to a subdivision]. So when I saw this episode with exaggerated subdivision atmosphere I found it ironic for it to air right then. (journal entry)

Everyone seemed scared by the idea of living in a gated community. Do young people not want to conform? (Jennifer FN, March 8)

Perhaps most heartening, many students said that they would now critically consider all of the implications of their own future home purchase decisions on various social formations (neighborhood, nation, "the environment," etc.) rather than follow the latest trend. In his journal Phil (from chapter 3's "Intervention Failed" spotlight box) concluded, "This entire episode reminded me strongly of something George Carlin said about how quick Americans are now to give up a portion of their freedom for convenience." In future entries he talked about how he increasingly doesn't want to be that kind of American. Indeed! A fun yet introspective salon centered on a show like *The X-Files* provides the participants with the space, time, and raw materials to pose and ponder difficult questions about themselves and their social worlds.

If I were doing this project again I would work with one of the next generation of sci-fi shows, such as the Sci-Fi channel's *Farscape*.[3] As was the case with my *X-Files* salon, groups of students would meet each week in an informal setting, and participants would also post messages to each other in a web-based electronic forum. As we have seen in other chapters, some students are more comfortable expressing themselves in a written medium than verbally, so this allows these individuals to fully participate in the discussion. Additionally, a supplemental forum allows the participants to expand on themes raised during face-to-face discussion, and introduce additional ideas for analysis.

As a new twist I would add engagement with a fan-based web site. For instance, while original episodes of the sci-fi show *Roswell* aired from 1999 to 2002, I frequently visited www.crashdown.com for the latest news and views on the show, which is about four extraterrestrial alien teenagers and their human friends/lovers. Members of a *Roswell* salon (the show appears currently in syndication) could compare their ideas with those found at crashdown.com. Before entry into the Pensieve many students assume that everyone thinks like them; participation in an on-line fan forum can expose them to a rich set of diverse ideas. My friends give me much grief about my love affair with *Roswell*—"How can a thirty-something black man like a show about whiney white teens?"—but I cannot resist a show with a host of ready-made social issues (such as alienation, the family, immigration, and sexuality) that are ripe for exploration by students not much older than the main characters.

Back to *The X-Files:* "whereas most mainstream television classically followed a very simplistic aesthetic strategy, *The X-Files* questions, undermines, and subverts conventional television codes, providing its own set of aesthetic pleasures" (Kellner 1999:164). It is, thus, an excellent source for creating Pensieves outside of classrooms, such as salons of students meeting in off-campus restaurants. In strange texts like *The X-Files*, "we are watching the conscious resignification of the metaphors that already dominate our view of the world around us. This resignification alerts us to the dangers of authority we have been taught to ignore and shows us a less dangerous path" (Bellon 1999:152). Such less dangerous paths can emerge when teachers create projects "establishing the pedagogical conditions for students to be able to develop a sense of perspective and hope in order to recognize that the way things are is not the way they have always been or must necessarily be in the future" (Giroux 2000:34). Using science-fiction texts in extracurricular Pensieves helps in this effort, as "science fiction is about the shadow that the future casts upon the present. It shows us how profoundly we are *haunted* by the ghosts of what has not yet happened" (Shaviro 2003:250; emphasis in original). Pensieves help us engage positive as well as negative manifestations of this condition.

Jennifer—"successful" intervention

As can be deduced from my decision to employ Jennifer as the spring semester autoethnography assistant and to involve her in the *X-Files* salon project, she was one of the fall semester students who embraced the purposes and lessons of a classroom as Pensieve. Let's take a brief look at her experiences while she was a student, starting with her reactions to the screening of the clip from the movie *I Like It Like That* (see chapter 3 for description):

I mostly want to focus on the issue of gender, though many other things about other issues could be said. A typical scenario occurred in the film, that being male dominance.

She wasn't "pretty" enough or from a good enough background to be considered anything by the dominant figure in the film, the male. She had to go out of her way to gain just a little respect, but still fell into a traditional female role of accepting whatever is eventually offered to her by the male, that being the job, instead of standing by her own will to survive without man's help. (first viewing critical reactions)

Critically, I truly cannot enjoy the clip that much. My biggest complaint is still the issue of gender roles. Again, the dominant oppressive male in the business world versus the little minority woman. True, she reacts well but the situation, I think, is comparable to oppressive societal gender roles. (second viewing critical reactions)

Finally, I'll consent to your idea of using other critical lenses to view this text! My main focus during this viewing was class, most definitely, considering the dialogue and actions between the two characters. The upper class male did not hold back with his criticism and ill-treatment of the lower class latino woman. With examples such as clothes, transportation (or lack thereof), living situations . . . all were critiqued by the upper class male toward the lower class female. Race, obviously, is also an issue. White is better than latino. However, Lisette does a great job of showing who the better person is, regardless of race. And gender . . . is obvious! (third viewing critical reactions)

Although she says that she has not entered the matrix of domination until the third viewing, she tentatively began to enter the matrix during the second reading by alluding to class ("the business world") and race ("the little minority woman"). An expansion beyond an exclusive focus on gender was also demonstrated in her media journals:

Week	Text	Focus
1	*Suburbia* (film)	youth culture
2	*Biography* article (magazine)	gender
3	*Melrose Place* (TV)	gender
4	*Law and Order* (TV)	gender
5	*Time* (magazine)	religion
6	campus newspaper article	race, gender
7	hip-hop/rap music	race, class
8	*In and Out* (film)	sexuality, gender
9	*Northern Exposure* (TV)	sexuality, gender
10	gURL (web site)	gender, class
11	ad in *US* (magazine)	class
12	MTV political program (TV)	youth culture

As can be seen, Jennifer also drew on a very wide variety of media genres (film, TV, magazines [articles and ads], newspapers, music, and the Internet)

for her journal entries, whereas most students used only two or three genres. In sum, Jennifer was an enthusiastic and dedicated student from the
first week; the class served mainly to broaden her interests in social critique from a focus strictly on gender politics to the intersections of multiple social formations (with gender still as a central component). She actual-
ized one of the key lessons I hoped to impart to the students: the necessity
of a flexible deployment of analytical tools to make sense of rapidly evolving social worlds.

Jennifer put these interests and skills to very effective use as my assistant
in the spring s101 "media and society" class and was an invaluable resource
as the assistant for the *X-Files* salon groups. She has indicated that these experiences were useful to her too; I hope that this is the case in her own
long line of future projects.

Assistants of the Pensieve

I do still believe that being a 494 was quite a bit of responsibility, and that the
students somewhat looked up to us, or at least saw us as more knowledgeable
or something, and I'm kind of glad I took it too seriously at the beginning. It
made me appreciate how hard it is to be in a position of authority, especially
because your expectations of yourself exceed the expectations others have of
you (most times). We are definitely our own worst critics. (Beeta, post-semester
project evaluation)

As we have seen, I used undergraduate assistants in both the autoethnography and follow-up *X-Files* salon project. I have also used undergraduate assistants before and after these two projects. Why use
undergraduates rather than graduate students? The presence of undergraduate assistants can help enrolled students see themselves as valuable members of the academic community: "If students see another
undergraduate participating in the responsibility of transmitting and
communicating knowledge, this can demonstrate the capacity of
undergraduates to actively participate in this process and break down
the notion that only an 'expert' faculty member has anything worth-
while to contribute to the class" (Fingerson and Culley 2001:311).
Undergraduate assistants help students more fully enter Pensieves.

At the end of the fall semester of the autoethnography I asked each
member of the 494 crew—Beeta, Rob, and Lori—to review their field
notes and provide summaries of themes they noted. One such theme was
the ways in which they were personally affected by the project. In general, they responded along the lines detailed in Beeta's reflection: did not

know how much work is involved in being in positions of authority, but learned to use that in positive ways, helping them understand their positionings better and increase their own agency. Although at a less conspicuous level than I, they were also "teachers as texts," and used reflection on their experiences to help the students as well as themselves.

Beeta notes that "I truly do not believe the class has turned me into a superanalytical critical perceiver of media in all its forms." As an ethnic minority, she continues, she was already attuned to the operation of difference in the media. She did, however, focus most of her scrutiny on race and ethnicity before joining the crew; throughout the semester she more fully entered the matrix of domination and looked at intersections of class and gender. In a field note from the third week of class, she notes that "I think about gender issues ONLY when other people point them out . . . just not part of my matrix of domination . . . I agree with Jennifer's point about supermom, but I would have never come to that conclusion myself . . . I like that, though . . . I do feel as if I'm being influenced in a positive manner . . . (today's the first day, though)."

Beeta also entered the class with an interesting enigma: although a double major in sociology and economics with an A average in both, she had a fear of not performing up to par in her 494 tasks: "I was soooo intimidated at first. I was horrified at the idea of running the EC, even if Lori was going to do most of the work." She did perform superbly throughout the semester, and "as far as my fear of failure goes, I would venture to say that it has improved throughout the semester." Indeed, Beeta's willingness to share insecurities as well as strengths may have been what endeared her to the students. As can be seen throughout this book, Beeta was the one the students most often talked to about class conduct.

Rob's field notes, on the other hand, were the least filled with correspondence with students. This suits the two of us just fine, though. As discussed in chapter 4, Rob was the most invested in a traditional ethnography, who wanted to observe dynamics that unfolded independently of any of his own specific actions. He did, however, develop more of a multisided view of "objectivity" and an appreciation of autoethnography, even if he would not necessarily conduct it himself: "it is crucial that one remains faithful to his own heart, mind, and soul. It is the voices of these which prompt us to stand up and say no to what we, with tempestuous conviction, know to be wrong. And which prompt us to stand firm and say yes to what we, with deep passion, know to be just."

Rob used this conviction to reconnect with a working-class urban past that he had left behind when he enrolled at Indiana University.

Through his s494 experiences as well as participation in other sociology and criminal justice classes, Rob has developed a nuanced understanding of inner-city social scapes. He wants to empower them through his work: "Having an insight of the urban youth subculture, that many sociologists, statesmen, and policy-makers lack, I hope one day I can transform the realities of my lived experience into a positive difference." Rob still has respect for traditional rational models of knowledge, but now desires an experiential-based supplement.

Lori also continued her ongoing efforts to powerfully articulate the personal and the political. With regard to media culture specifically, she writes that "I honestly cannot say that this class has changed my relation to media culture in either a good or bad way. Having had Walt in class two other times, not to mention the numerous outside of class discussions we've had, much of the material presented was review. That, in addition to the fact that I've been extremely analytical of media for several years now, leads me to doubt that s101 has shaped my thinking; perhaps polishing would be a more accurate description." She described part of such polishing in her last posting in the fall EC:

this really was quite an interesting semester on many levels, and i found much value in observing the various ways in which many of you became more critical as time went on. . . . on a personal level, i initially found it very difficult to make the transition from helping walt with his race and ethnicity class (for which i was his TA last semester) to working with material that dealt with more inclusive examinations of media representations. ultimately, i shifted gears and came to appreciate the opportunity to address gender and class related issues, both of which are deep concerns of mine. having said this, however, i would encourage you all to use this class as a stepping stone that will hopefully lead to more thorough understandings of all the issues we discussed. while walt did a fantastic job of addressing so many of our current societal dilemmas, there was simply not enough time to fully explore all of them. some of you have mentioned an interest in taking more sociology courses, and i would certainly recommend that you do so. the Afro-American Studies and Gender Studies depts. would also be excellent spaces in which to continue the dialogue initiated by this class. but even if academia doesn't have a hand in it, i truly hope that we continue to increase our critical literacy throughout our lives.

A concluding note about the 494 crew in general was that their presence was an invaluable aspect of the autoethnography. I thank them for their willingness to share criticism as well as praise of components of all levels of the project. They have definitely facilitated the creation of the classroom as Pensieve.

While Jennifer was not part of "the 494 crew" she did receive three hours of credit for sociology s494 for serving as the undergraduate assistant in the spring. While not as extensive as the training involved for the 494 crew, I gave her a guide for taking field notes and a copy of my field notes from the first day of the fall, and we discussed issues of auto-ethnography throughout the semester in our weekly working lunches, during which we also reviewed our notes for the week and any other pertinent issues.

Like the 494 crew, I asked Jennifer to write a summary of her experiences on the project. She begins by stating that "to say that the impact on my life from participating in the s494 project was great would be a giant understatement. There are so many factors that made s494 a special and meaningful, as well as difficult and thought-provoking, time in my life." She goes on to talk about creating new perspectives on issues such as diversity, tolerance, bias, and academic research in general. She was a double major in sociology and gender studies, but notes that exposure to the project "has shifted my focus a bit from specifically gender studies to cultural studies, which encompasses so many more issues that I am truly interested in."

As was the case with Beeta, Jennifer's positioning within the matrix of domination has shifted, as she's added race and class to complement her strong understanding and commitment to gender: "I didn't mind that [Walt] told everyone that I am a feminist—I actually loved it that he made this fact known. So many people are afraid of that word and are scared to label themselves as such. By being open about that conviction, I was able to hopefully prove that is possible for a reasonable, level-headed woman to be a feminist." Indeed, like the 494 crew, Jennifer was a teacher as text.

Anna was also not part of the 494 crew itself, but was instrumental in advancing the project. Like Jennifer, she was a student in the fall class, and received sociology s494 credit in the spring: one hour for sitting in on three of the spring classes and taking notes on differences between that class and the fall class. I have referred to these notes in previous chapters; they were important in sketching the general theme of the different inflections on critical literacy. In her summary she writes, "last semester I was not ready for class to end because it seemed like the class didn't get to show their full critical and sharing potential. This [spring] class obviously was more involved and created a better learning environment."

During the year Anna was also involved in a collaborative graduate-undergraduate research program on the applicability of sociological understandings of "alienation" in postindustrial America. That study used a phone survey; the three undergraduate assistants learned about survey methodology in general and participated in phone interviews conducted by Indiana University's Center for Survey Research. At the time Anna was thinking about going to graduate school in sociology, but was unsure about potential methodologies to employ, so I asked her to compare survey and ethnographic methods. She concluded that "[Ethnography] is much more personal and allows the researcher to make more personal conclusions. It isn't cut and dried and that is good. Complicated, but good. . . . You definitely have to have lots of self-confidence to do this type of observation. You have to hold confidence that your conclusions are valid although you can't back them up with a bunch of numbers." Like Jennifer and Beeta, Anna specifically mentions an increase in personal self-confidence and better understanding of sociological research in general.

In sum, serving as a teaching and/or research assistant can be just as valuable for the assistant as it can be for the instructor, who gains more eyes, ears, and hands. Assistants gain insights into institutional workings of structures like the Academy, which helps them think about possible career choices and goals (Jacobs 2002). I should add that these insights are gained most often through informal contact with faculty and staff. Over the years assistants and I have eaten meals together, watched TV and movies, and even jointly played on intramural basketball teams. Most of the assistants and I believe that we've learned as much from each other (if not more) in informal activities as in official instructor-assistant business.

In interaction (formal as well as informal) with the instructor the assistants see firsthand what it takes to be a professor, and the professor learns fresh perspectives from energetic young scholars. Enrolled students, in turn, also benefit from the richer set of experiences and strategies deployed. Instructors and assistants help each individual in a Pensieve function as a "critical organic catalyst" (West 1990:40): "A person who stays attuned to the best of what the mainstream has to offer—its paradigms, viewpoints, and methods—yet maintains a grounding in affirming and enabling subcultures of criticism." In classrooms as Pensieves we need such individuals in order to help all the participants (students, assistants, and instructors) continually articulate disparate mediated fragments of multiple issues and events to carve out more powerful, if fleeting, social realities. We need to continually conjure such spaces throughout the Academy . . . and beyond.

Chapter Seven

Evoking the Lower Frequencies

Spectators are not the dupes of the media theater, but they refuse to say so.
— MICHEL DE CERTEAU, *Culture in the Plural*

I used this passage from Michel de Certeau's *Culture in the Plural* in chapter 1 to set up the overview of this book. Let me invoke it again to wrap up the book, as a guide for some concluding remarks about what happens when we create college classrooms as Pensieves. Aaron Schutz (2004:17) argues that "while students may develop quite sophisticated understandings of how forms of oppression affect them directly, they may have little or no knowledge of the larger social, cultural, and institutional systems that support this treatment." Amy Lee (2000:5) further notes that "it is not enough to *have* visions [of critical pedagogies], we need also to consider the contexts and conditions that foster or constrain our efforts to *realize* them."[1] This book shows how teachers can help students create sociological imaginations to understand both personal troubles and larger social and cultural issues as created by and/or disseminated through electronic mass media.

The 1997–1998 autoethnography and 1998–1999 *X-Files* salon project were experimental interventions seeking evidence for the effects of alternative pedagogy on critical literacy; they investigated what happens when students are encouraged to say that they are not dupes of the media. Students participated in Pensieves where they learned to evoke the lower frequencies, exploring ideas and experiences that usually remain in the background. They learned to say that they were active negotiators of various social ideas, and used this voice inside and outside of media culture classes.

My attempt to create Pensieves did not, of course, end with late 1990s autoethnographies and salons at Indiana University. Schutz (2004:21) argues, "[i]f educators hope to foster a more equitable society through their efforts . . . then they cannot avoid thinking more carefully about the pluses and minuses involved in different ways of understanding domination and resistance." In this chapter I will discuss recent nuances I've learned about the possibilities and problematics of college classrooms as Pensieves. Specifically, I will explore a cautionary tale learned in the fall of 2000 while using the *Space Traders* strange text; a spring 2001 twist on the use of undergraduate teaching assistants; and the "Educational Storytelling Project," a pedagogical technique created in spring 2002.[2] Finally, I will conclude with a brief look at the possibilities afforded us by an unusual definition of "evocation." In the end, this book is only the beginning.

Another Look at *Space Traders*

In chapter 4 I discussed my use of the strange text *Space Traders,* the forty-minute film that explores an alien proposal to exchange all African Americans for new technologies and wealth. I use the film in all my sociology classes, from ones dealing specifically with race to general "Introduction to Sociology" courses. During the 2000–2001 academic year I taught a "Living in the Electronic Information Age" freshman seminar, focusing on the rapidly changing roles of electronic technology in society. Aside from a change in topic from "media" to "technology," and a greatly reduced class size (mid-sixties to fifteen students), my experiences with the freshman seminar and the "media and society" courses of the 1997–1998 autoethnography were similar in the overall result: I created a classroom as Pensieve in which the undergraduate students explored flexible and contingent understandings of new and old experiences and knowledges. There is, however, one result from the 2000–2001 year that illustrates a glaring omission in my use of "the teacher as text" to create a Pensieve, one that provides a cautionary lesson: it is not always the students who resist critical literacy; sometimes it is us, despite our best intentions.

I screened *Space Traders* in both semesters of the freshman seminar. Whereas I focused on the media and mediated aspects of the film in the 1997–1998 "media and society" classes, in the freshman seminar I concentrated on the cultural aspects of the technologies that were depicted in the film, such as the promise of an unlimited power source. Unlike in the autoethnography, however, the freshman seminar students did not further investigate the text outside of classes. I did not assign an essay on the film, and few students discussed it in the EC. In the fall of 2000, for instance, only three students discussed the topic in the "coffee house" section of the EC, where students voluntarily initiated topics (normally there were five to ten responses to a coffee house topic). The three postings are as follows:

What if that movie had the aliens asking minorities to take all white people? Do you think it would have a higher probability of happening? Do you think that technology is or will be so important that we will be willing to trade lives for it?

I think that if the aliens wanted to take all white people, it would have fallen through. First of all, in the movie, most of the people that were being proposed by the idea from the aliens were white . . . like the white president of the United States was gonna let that happen! Secondly, I think there would've been major riots. Even though I think it didn't happen in the movie, if it were to happen in real life, whether it was whites or blacks, one of the groups would've rioted on the other because of jealousy of being forced to leave and / or discrimination. As far as trading lives goes, I think a lot of Americans today are more family-orientated, religious, and have more morals installed in their heads, than they did back in the day. So to answer this question, I don't think technology will ever get to the point where people are willing to risk another life—it wouldn't be humane.

I don't think that whites would have been sent away . . . or blacks . . . or anyone. Maybe I am being a little optimistic, but I think that the world is much better than that. There would be no way that such a racist act would be able to go through so easily. There would be huge riots all over the world, not only from blacks, but whites, and any other minorities. The place would be chaotic. What I wanted to also discuss was when London (I think) supposedly offered "their" blacks too! What the heck is that? This would not be possible at all! They were talking about blacks as things as if they owned them. It was just crazy! There may still be racism, but I don't think it is so severe that such an event could ever take place.

In the fall 2000 freshman seminar five of the fourteen students were students of color. All three postings were by students of color, and of particular interest is the fact that the two responses to the original posting were by Asian Americans. As both of these students insist that the trade would not happen in real life, one could argue that they were under the sway of the "myth of the model minority," which teaches us that Asian Americans "mistakenly believed that they would be taken care of if they worked hard, did not complain, and contributed hand-somely to powerful political figures. . . . [But] a model minority is expe-diently forgotten and dismissed if white dominance or security is threatened" (Cho 1993:202). I did not take up the challenge of discuss-ing the complexities of the "model minority" thesis with the students, either in class or in the next class period after the EC postings.

I did not discuss the postings in later class periods because the once-a-week seminar was on to completely different topics by the time the messages appeared, and I wanted to sustain interests in the new topics rather than rehash old ground. During the *Space Traders* class, however, why did I not explicitly investigate the "model minority" myth with the students, given that I have outlined it in other *Space Traders* discus-sions? Simply put, the extensive presence of Asian American students (30% of the class) dissuaded me, as I never before had more than a smattering of these students in classes so I did not know how a poten-tially explosive personal topic for many Asian Americans could unfold, and I thus veered to more familiar territory. Of course, if one of the stu-dents had raised the topic I would have engaged it, but the point here is that I did not introduce a potentially powerful topic because it pushed me too far out of my own comfort level.

In chapter 4 I analyzed my fears and frustrations regarding the African American experience as highlighted by *Space Traders*, some-thing that is very familiar to me. To create a truly powerful Pensieve, however, teachers should also be willing to explore unknown dangers when they sense that such an exploration can be beneficial to the class. In this instance I ignored an inkling to that effect, but wish that I hadn't. I have not yet had another experience that tempts me to back away from a new and troubling in-class development, but when it happens I hope that I will not be afraid to engage. This is especially important in a post-September 11 world, where "[a]s concerned citizens, we are re-quired to understand more fully why the tools we used in the past often feel awkward in the present" (Giroux 2003:xvii).

Using Lower-Division Teaching Assistants

In the Indiana University autoethnography and *X-Files* salon project I used advanced undergraduate teaching/research assistants: Anna, Beeta, Lori, and Rob were seniors and Jennifer was a second-semester junior (and senior during the *X-Files* project). At the University of Min-nesota I am a faculty member in a unit that works almost exclusively with first and second year students, so I have experimented with using lower-division teaching assistants (freshman and sophomores) in classes as Pensieves, finding that these assistants are invaluable in helping young students build constructive understandings of the ways of life of college students and learn strategies for being productive and successful in various student cultures (Jacobs 2002). As with advanced assistants, when lower-division students work as assistants, they gain valuable practice in critically reflecting on their own beliefs, experiences, and skills in order to assist other students in the same process.

Fingerson and Culley (2001) note that students—on all levels of the undergraduate spectrum—usually only comment on the performance of undergraduate teaching assistants (TAs) when problems arise, and don't provide feedback on course evaluations unless specifically instructed. My experiences have been similar. I therefore specifically asked the students in TA Jocelyn Gutzman's spring semester 2001 "Introduction to Sociology" class an open-ended question about her performance ("What did you think of having an undergraduate as your TA?") on the anonymous course evaluation. Forty students were enrolled in the course, and about thirty were in attendance on the last day of class. Twenty-six students answered the question about the TA, and the only criticism was from four students who, while expressing the opinion that Jocelyn did a good job, wished that she were even more involved in the class. All others only listed positive reactions. Most interestingly, twelve students mentioned that Jocelyn was valuable because she was close to them in age and therefore understood their experiences and concerns. A typical response in this set was along the lines of the following student's comment:

Jocelyn was a very good TA. She knew the material very well. I think that it's a good idea to have an undergraduate for a TA because they understand how we feel and know what we are going through. Jocelyn put up very reasonable questions in the EC. She is there when we need her help. I think that you should have TAs in all your classes, Walt!

Of the twelve students who commented on Jocelyn's age as an asset to them, there is a particularly interesting subset in which three students believe that an undergraduate TA is a good model for other students, and one of these responses includes a belief that an assistantship is also valuable for the TA. This subset is listed below:

I think that having Jocelyn as a TA was very helpful for the class as well as for herself. It gave us some inspiration to have a TA close to our own age and could help us out on activities.

Having Jocelyn as a TA was a wonderful idea. She made everything more clear in the EC. And also I think it is good to have somebody like her to look upon and see what it is like in future college years. She set a good example for us undergraduate freshmen, by showing us what to expect from college.

My thoughts on Jocelyn being a TA were basically things that were good. It gave the class, I think, a sense of comfort, to relax and not be all uptight about things. It showed to me that even students like ourselves could do the things she does in the future, and I think by having her around made the class more fun.

Finally, one response states that "I felt more comfortable in confronting her and asking questions compared to my other TAs who were not undergraduate students." Consequently,the presence of an undergraduate TA can provide a resource that is otherwise not used by some students. Obviously, however, not all students thought that a TA is a necessary resource. For instance, one student wrote, "I guess I didn't communicate with Jocelyn enough to develop an opinion about her," and we don't know the opinion of the fourteen people who did not complete course evaluations. In sum, though, the majority of the students who did complete the evaluations expressed the opinion that a lower-division undergraduate TA is beneficial to their development. Once again, we see that assistants are integral components of creating college classrooms as Pensieves.

The Educational Storytelling Project

To write stories concerning exclusions and invisibilities is to write ghost stories. To write ghost stories implies that ghosts are real, that is to say, that they produce material effects. To impute a kind of objectivity to ghosts implies that, from certain standpoints, the dialectics of visibility and invisibility involve a constant negotiation between what can be seen and what is in the shadows. —AVERY GORDON, *Ghostly Matters*

As part of the 1997–1998 autoethnography I read short stories to each class and led discussion about some of the implications of various storytelling activities in the social construction of their ideas and experiences (see chapter 5). In 2002 I developed another storytelling technique—the Educational Storytelling Project (ESP)—to help students investigate the construction of their worlds, centered on "ghosts" (of a social versus paranormal kind), the strong but usually unconscious forces that shape our everyday lives. Working with ghost stories provides students with another interesting way to push through their taken-for-granted, commonsense ideas to reveal the history that makes the social world function in particular ways and the processes that sustain or challenge those functions; engaging ghost stories sharpens students' sociological imaginations.

Gordon (1997:8) argues that in confronting social ghosts we learn that our worlds are not as simple as they first appear: "haunting describes how that which appears to be not there is often a seething presence, acting on and often meddling with taken-for-granted realities . . . investigating [ghosts] can lead to that dense site where history and subjectivity make social life." In order to reach these sites I had each student in my 2002 "Introduction to Sociology" classes (a) write a short ghost story, (b) read it orally in a small group, and (c) write a reflection on another student's story and performance. Students also had the option of presenting their ESP story to the entire class. Finally, the class collectively analyzed the project in a discussion I facilitated.

One ghost that many students investigated was that of language—how we often unconsciously use certain words or phrases to stigmatize groups (prevent them from obtaining full societal acceptance and participation). For instance, students will use the phrase "that's gay" to signal disapproval or dislike. In his ESP story to the entire class, one student, John, came out as a gay man, centering on the pain he feels when reminded about marginalization. In his reflection John noted,

When each of us is pulled apart for some factor that we have no control over, it makes us debate many things, including how valuable we are as people. From writing stories like these people have to think how deep they would like to go in their writing, and what may be too personal for the reader versus what might be too personal for the writer to talk about.

John went on to talk about how he wanted to explicitly use his ESP story to raise awareness about issues of difference, specifically related to sexual orientation. Many students are reluctant to consider life experiences of those different from themselves, so they will often grudgingly read assigned articles about various minority groups and only a few will participate in class discussion (and usually these students are members of the topic group). The ESP provides a framework in which students can get outside of themselves and stretch their sociological imaginations. In reflection papers several students commented on John's coming-out experience. One student wrote, "this ESP project allowed me to look into myself and find socializing agents that make me who I am today. And, it also caused me to gain a newfound respect for gays and lesbians," while another stated: "thinking about social ghosts makes me want to be more understanding. I have so many social ghosts that it makes me sure that everyone has at least a few that affect them all the time. I think it would be good for everyone to realize that everyone has these issues and to be aware of them and treat people accordingly." In other words, students gain an understanding of stigma and its effects.[3]

John concluded his reflection by stating, "in my ESP story, I thought a lot about what I've learned from being a homosexual male, and tried to talk about my schooling, and the many ways and things I learned throughout because of it." Another student wrote, "to be honest I never really looked at how my social status affected my writing or my performance style. Now that I've had a chance to look and analyze this concept I noticed a lot about myself and my creative expression." Many other students sounded similar themes of introspection in their papers. Indeed, the use of tools such as the ESP encourage all students to take more responsibility for their learning, in the process helping each other create powerful learning strategies in college classrooms as Pensieves.

Evocation as Beginning

In essence, all my projects seek to chart the processes and products of a pedagogy in which instructors and students use mediated mass-market objects, images, sounds, and words to create and live malleable postmodern social worlds where individuals "sample, they appropriate, they hybridize, they distort, they remix and recombine" (Shaviro 2003:59). I want to evoke, to "call into being something that was absent; it is a coming to be of what was neither there present nor absent, for we are not to understand 'evocation' as linking two differences in time and place, as something that evokes and something else evoked" (Tyler 1986:130).

Creating the college classroom as Pensieve details the planning, conduct, and results of deliberate "controlled chaos," the introduction of multiple perspectives, experiences, texts, emotions, dreams, fears, hopes, and desires in an effort to help all involved think differently about their social worlds. It invites all to become "critical social agents" (McLaren 1995:15 and 56):

Living as a critical social agent means knowing how to live contingently and provisionally without the certainty of knowing the truth, yet at the same time with the courage to take a stand on issues of human suffering, domination, and oppression. . . . As postmodern dreamers, it has become our burden as well as our responsibility to transform our despair into compassion and commitment, to challenge our feelings of disorientation and hopelessness with an ethics of risk and refusal.

Living as critical social agents helps us juxtapose Gilroy's (1993:37) "politics of fulfillment, the notion that a future society will be able to realize the social and political promise that present society has left unaccomplished," and a "politics of transfiguration, [which] points specifically to the formation of a community of needs and solidarity which is magically made audible in [creative articulation of ideas and dreams] and is palpable in the social relations of its cultural utility and reproduction." I try to teach students how to use media and its products to juxtapose existing ideas of society and themselves with new subaltern ones, and to strive to continually evolve their consciousness. In this effort,

The politics of fulfillment is mostly content to play occidental rationality at its own game. It necessitates a hermeneutic orientation that can assimilate the semiotic, the verbal, and textual. The politics of transfiguration strives in pursuit of the sublime, struggling to repeat the unrepresentable. Its rather different hermeneutic focus pushes towards the mimetic, dramatic, and performative (Gilroy 1993:37).

I attempt to suspend these two hermeneutics in constructive tension: by creating college classrooms as Pensieves, the participants (instructors as well as students) all learn to combine the visible and invisible, the said and the unsaid, in ways that potentially make our social worlds more open, nuanced, pleasurable, and just. We learn that "simply stated, schools are not neutral institutions designed for providing students with work skills or with the privileged tools of culture. Instead, they are deeply implicated in forms of inclusion and exclusion that produce particular moral truths and values. In effect, they both produce and legitimate cultural differences as part of their broader project of constructing particular knowledge/power relations and producing specific notions of citizenship" (Giroux 1993:373). We create strategies of using knowledge/power relations to strive for other possibilities.

bell hooks (1994a:207) closes *Teaching to Transgress* with thoughts on the classroom as location of possibility:

The academy is not paradise. But learning is a place where paradise can be created. The classroom, with all its limitations, remains a location of possibility. In that field of possibility we have the opportunity to labor for freedom, to demand of ourselves and our comrades, an openness of mind and heart that allows us to face reality even as we collectively imagine ways to move beyond boundaries, to transgress. This is education as the practice of freedom.

When we engage education as the practice of freedom we can create the college classroom as a Pensieve. In this simultaneously terrifying and thrilling project we continually call new understandings and practices into formation, based on the shifting articulations of past, present, and future dreams and structures. Cross into that space with me. . . .

Notes

Chapter 1

1. Guy Trombley introduced the idea of using the Pensieve as a metaphor for the classroom in "Interactive Class Websites as Research Tools: Student-Driven Meta-Analysis and Evaluation of Students' Learning Process," a paper presented at the 2001 *Classrooms of the Future* conference (Minneapolis, MN).

2. Paul Gilroy (2000:127) advises us to "remember and adapt Marx's insight: we make our own identities, but with inherited resources and not under circumstances of our own choosing."

3. See Merton (1973) on the palimpsest as a metaphor, and Clifford and Marcus (1986) on the crisis of representation.

Chapter 2

1. For additional insights into the process of articulation, see parts I and II of *Stuart Hall: Critical Dialogues in Cultural Studies* (Routledge, 1996), especially essays by Dick Hebdige ("Postmodernism and 'The Other Side'") and Jennifer Slack ("The Theory and Method of Articulation in Cultural Studies").

2. The "sociological imagination" is the ability to connect personal experiences with larger societal events and issues. See chapter 3 for a full discussion.

3. Originally I selected four students. The fourth student dropped out of the project halfway through the fall semester, due to personal issues.

4. Lori and Beeta both construct identities in accordance with McLaren's (1995:126–128) "resistance multiculturalism," which argues that appreciation of diversity must be linked with a commitment to social justice. See also the Bad Subject Production Team's (1998:12) distinction of "critical multiculturalism" from "vulgar multiculturalism," and Bruch et al's (2004:13–14) discussion of "celebratory," "critical," and "transformative" approaches to multiculturalism.

Chapter 3

1. Over the course of the semester thirteen students dropped the course in the fall (out of an initial enrollment of seventy-eight), and eight dropped in the spring (out of seventy-four on the first roster).

2. With the exception of the assistants (Lori, Beeta, Rob, Jennifer, and Anna), all student names are pseudonyms.

3. The fall class had sixty-five students on the final roster: twenty-four freshmen, twenty-two sophomores, eight juniors, and eleven seniors. Sixty-six students were enrolled on the last roster of the spring class: nine freshmen, nineteen sophomores, fifteen juniors, and twenty-three seniors.

4. There were a total of nine comments about the Gap ad. Additionally, the Allen-Edmonds ad had eight comments, the Sega ad had six, McDonald's and Simple ads both had five comments, and three comments were posted about the Mercedes advertisement.

Chapter 4

1. For a more complete discussion of the film's representations of compliance and resistance, see Dwight Brooks and Walter Jacobs, "Black Men in the Margins" [*Communication Studies* 47(1996):289–302].

2. The designation "ABC" is a pseudonym.

3. The fall class had forty-six lower-division students (out of a total enrollment of sixty-five), whereas the spring class was taken by only twenty-eight (of sixty-six) of these first- and second-year students. Additionally, note that one of the freshmen and four of the sophomores in the spring class were nontraditional returning students over the age of thirty.

4. During an office visit they told me that they learned quite a bit more the second time around.

5. See Hennessy 1995, Phelan 1995, Seidman 1995, and Warner 1993 for general discussions of queer theory. See Anzaldua 1997, Berube and Berube 1997, Chabram-Dernersesian 1997, Davy 1997, Hill 2004, and Sandell 1997 for intersections of queer sexuality and whiteness.

Chapter 5

1. "The Story-Teller" is about a bachelor telling an "improper story" to two young children when their aunt fails to keep them amused while on a long train ride. During the class discussion of October 8, 1997, Lori noted: "Jennifer says it has gender implications in that woman was dismissed as prudish old disciplinarian, while man was regarded as engaging and stimulating. Excellent point, one that I would've made had she not."

2. For a discussion of how sexual orientation can be engaged more successfully, see Heather Hartley's "What's My Orientation? Using the Teacher-as-Text Strategy as Feminist Pedagogical Practice" [*Teaching Sociology* 27 (1999): 398–406].

3. In any one class (of both semesters of the 1997–1998 autoethnography) up to half of the students would talk while others listened. Overall, roughly a third of students would speak at least once a week, those in a second third would

speak every two or three weeks, and members of the final third would usually just listen.

4. In my third year of graduate school I took a class called "Representations of the Postmodern," taught by a white lesbian renowned for theorizing intersections of race and sexuality. As the lone person of color in the room I was, surprisingly, expected to provide "expert analysis" during a week on race; simultaneously, however, the instructor and my classmates realized that this was a position that I should not have been put in. That tension literally paralyzed the discussion: we danced around issues and everyone left the class uneasy. The next class was no better, as we fumbled with not only a discussion of the topic, but also with a meta-narrative of what happened in the previous class.

5. The second round of Kiva sessions was also instrumental in developing the foundation for the final project I used in both classes of the 1997–1998 autoethnography. In all his sessions Rob asked the students about "inspirational" movies; after the session with Pam and Eliza I developed guidelines that I still use in many of my classes today. Each student picks a media product that the student regards as "inspirational," experiences it with another person who is socially different, and analyzes why they agree or disagree about the articulations they have individually and collectively generated.

Chapter 6

1. The Indiana Institutional Review Board (IRB) made a number of suggestions that improved my research techniques. Following J. Michael Oakes (2002), I recommend that all researchers submit plans to their local IRB for review, even if not required.

2. See chapter 5 of Douglas Kellner's *Media Spectacle* (Routledge, 2003). Many fans hated the last two seasons of the show, which featured little of founding character Fox Mulder. I, however, was a die-hard fan of *The X-Files* all the way up (down?) to its May 2002 demise.

3. Here is tvguide.com's description of *Farscape:* "A freak accident during an experimental space mission throws astronaut John Crichton (Ben Browder) thousands of light-years across the galaxy, into an alien battlefield where he joins a band of extraterrestrial refugees." Sadly, *Farscape* was cancelled in 2003. Many of the episodes are available on DVD, and the series creators produced a syndicated mini-series in 2004. They may also film a movie version, as did the producers of *The X-Files* (releasing *The X-Files: Fight the Future* in the summer of 1998).

Chapter 7

1. Emphasis is in the original. Lee's *Composing Critical Pedagogies* (NCTE 2000) is "a project . . . to consider what it means not only to claim but to enact a pedagogy" (p. 5). My book is written in that spirit.

2. These techniques were deployed at the University of Minnesota—Twin Cities.

3. Mark Pedelty (2001:67) argues that "it is crucial that we make the discussion of stigma and other important cultural realities part of our research and teaching agenda. How can we hope to positively transform our institutions if we do not fully explore the students' experience within them and attitudes toward them?"

Bibliography

Alexander, Bryant. 1999. "Performing Culture in the Classroom: An Instructional (Auto)Ethnography." *Text and Performance Quarterly* 19:307–331.

Anderson, Elijah. 1990. *Streetwise: Race, Class, and Change in an Urban Community*. Chicago: University of Chicago Press.

Anderson, Gary L., and Patricia Irvine. 1993. "Informing Critical Literacy with Ethnography." Pp. 81–104 in C. Lankshear and P. McLaren (eds.), *Critical Literacy: Politics, Praxis, and the Postmodern*. Albany: State University of New York Press.

Anderson, Margaret L., and Patricia Hill Collins (eds.). 1998. *Race, Class, and Gender: An Anthology,* 3rd ed. New York: Wadsworth.

Anzaldua, Gloria. 1987. *Borderlands/La Frontera: The New Mestiza*. San Francisco: Aunt Lute.

Apple, Michael. 2000. *Official Knowledge: Democratic Education in a Conservative Age,* 2nd ed. New York: Routledge.

Aronowitz, Stanley. 2000. *The Knowledge Factory: Dismantling the Corporate University and Creating True Higher Learning*. Boston: Beacon.

Babcock, Barbara. 1980. "Reflexivity: Definitions and Discriminations." *Semiotica* 30:1–14.

Bad Subjects Production Team. 1998. *Bad Subjects: Political Education for Everyday Life*. New York: New York University Press.

Balsamo, Anne. 1997. *Technologies of the Gendered Body: Reading Cyborg Women*. Durham, NC: Duke University Press.

Bartky, Sandra. 1990. *Femininity and Domination: Studies in the Phenomenology of Oppression*. New York: Routledge.

Baudrillard, Jean. 1994. *Simulacra and Simulation*. Ann Arbor: University of Michigan Press.

Baudrillard, Jean. 1988. *America*. London: Verso.

Baudrillard, Jean. 1983. "The Ecstasy of Communication." Pp. 126–134 in H. Foster (ed.), *The Anti-Aesthetic: Essays on Postmodern Culture*. Seattle: Bay Press.

Beatty, Paul. 1996. *The White Boy Shuffle*. New York: Houghton-Mifflin.

Bell, Derrick. 1992. *Faces at the Bottom of the Well: The Permanence of Racism*. New York: Basic Books.

Bellon, Joe. 1999. "The Strange Discourse of *The X-Files:* What it is, What it does, and What is at stake." *Critical Studies in Mass Communication* 16(2):136–154.

Berman, Paul (ed.). 1994. *Blacks and Jews: Alliances and Arguments*. New York: Delacorte.

Berube, Alan, and Florence Berube. 1997. "Sunset Trailer Park." Pp. 15–40 in M. Wray and A. Newitz (eds.), *White Trash: Race and Class in America*. New York: Routledge.

Bobo, Jacqueline. 1995. *Black Women as Cultural Readers*. New York: Columbia University Press.

Bochner, Arthur, and Carolyn Ellis. 2001. *Ethnographically Speaking: Autoethnography, Literature, and Aesthetics*. Walnut Creek, CA: AltaMira Press.

Brooks, Dwight E., and Walter R. Jacobs. 1996. "Black Men in the Margins: *Space Traders* and the Interpositional Fight Against B[l]acklash." *Communication Studies* 47:289–302.

Bruch, Patrick L., Rashne R. Jehangir, Walter R. Jacobs, and David L. Ghere. 2004. "Enabling Access: Toward Multicultural Developmental Curricula." *Journal of Developmental Education* 27(3):12–19, 41.

Calhoun, Craig (ed.). 1992. *Habermas and the Public Sphere*. Cambridge: The MIT Press.

Carter, Chris (producer). 1999. "Arcadia," *The X-Files* episode 6X13 (video recording). New York: Fox Television Network.

Carter, Chris (producer and director). 1997. "Post-Modern Prometheus," *The X-Files* episode 5X06 (video recording). New York: Fox Television Network.

Chabram-Dernersesian, Angie. 1997. "On the Social Construction of Whiteness within Selected Chicano/a Discourses." Pp. 107–164 in R. Frankenberg (ed.), *Displacing Whiteness: Essays in Social and Cultural Criticism*. Durham, NC: Duke University Press.

Cho, Sumi. 1993. "Korean Americans vs. African Americans: Conflict and Construction." Pp. 196–211 in R. Gooding-Williams (ed.), *Reading Rodney King, Reading Urban Uprising*. New York: Routledge.

Clifford, James, and George Marcus (eds.). 1986. *Writing Culture: The Poetics and Politics of Ethnography*. Berkeley: University of California Press.

Clough, Patricia. 1992. *The End(s) of Ethnography: From Realism to Social Criticism*. Newbury Park, CA: Sage.

Collins, Patricia Hill. 1991. *Black Feminist Thought: Knowledge, Consciousness, and the Politics of Empowerment*. New York: Routledge.

Connell, R. W. 1995. *Masculinities*. Berkeley: University of California Press.

Corsaro, Bill. 1985. *Friendship and Peer Culture in the Early Years*. Norwood, NJ: Ablex.

Davy, Kate. 1997. "Outing Whiteness: A Feminist/Lesbian Project." Pp. 204–225 in M. Hill (ed.), *Whiteness: A Critical Reader*. New York: New York University Press.

de Certeau, Michel. 1997/1974. *Culture in the Plural*. Minneapolis: University of Minnesota Press.

Dellucchi, Michael, and Kathleen Korgen. 2002. "'We're the Customer—We Pay the Tuition': Student Consumerism among Undergraduate Sociology Majors." *Teaching Sociology* 30(1):100–107.

Dellucchi, Michael, and William Smith. 1997a. "A Postmodern Explanation of Student Consumerism in Higher Education." *Teaching Sociology* 25:322–327.

Dellucchi, Michael, and William Smith. 1997b. "Satisfied Customers Versus

Pedagogic Responsibility: Further Thoughts on Student Consumerism."
Teaching Sociology 25:336–337.

Denzin, Norman. 1997. *Interpretive Ethnography: Ethnographic Practices for the 21st Century*. Thousand Oaks, CA: Sage.

Dover, Jay, and Viveca Greene. 1997. "The Media Literacy Antidote." Pp. 69–71 in D. Hazen and J. Winokur (eds.), *We the Media: A Citizens' Guide to Fighting for Media Democracy*. New York: The New Press.

du Gay, Paul, Stuart Hall, Linda Janes, Hugh Mackay, and Keith Negus. 1997. *Doing Cultural Studies: The Story of the Sony Walkman*. London: Sage.

Dumont, Clayton. 1995. "Toward a Multicultural Sociology: Bringing Postmodernism into the Classroom." *Teaching Sociology* 23:307–320.

Duneier, Mitchell. 1992. *Slim's Table: Race, Respectability, and Masculinity*. Chicago: University of Chicago Press.

Eco, Umberto. 1994. *Six Walks in the Fictional Woods*. Cambridge: Harvard University Press.

Eisenberg, Anne. 1997. "Education and the Marketplace: Conflicting Arenas? Response to 'A Postmodern Explanation of Student Consumerism in Higher Education.'" *Teaching Sociology* 25:328–332.

Ellis, Carolyn, and Arthur P. Bochner. 1996. *Composing Ethnography: Alternative Forms of Qualitative Writing*. Walnut Creek, CA: AltaMira Press.

Ellis, Carolyn, and Arthur P. Bochner. 1994. "Telling and Performing Personal Stories: The Constraints of Choice in Abortion." Pp. 79–101 in C. Ellis and M. Flaherty (eds.), *Investigating Subjectivity: Research on Lived Experience*. Newbury Park, CA: Sage.

Ellison, Ralph. 1989/1952. *Invisible Man*. New York: Vintage.

Faludi, Susan. 1991. *Backlash: The Undeclared War Against American Women*. New York: Anchor Books.

Feagan, Joe R., Hernan Vera, and Nikitah Imani. 1996. *The Agony of Education: Black Students at White Colleges and Universities*. New York: Routledge.

Fingerson, Laura, and Aaron Culley. 2001. "Collaborators in Learning: Undergraduate Teaching Assistants in the Classroom." *Teaching Sociology* 29(3):299–315.

Fiske, John. 1994a. *Media Matters: Everyday Culture and Political Change*. Minneapolis: University of Minnesota Press.

Fiske, John. 1994b. "Audiencing: Cultural Practice and Cultural Studies." Pp. 189–198 in N. Denzin and Y. Lincoln (eds.), *Handbook of Qualitative Research*. Thousand Oaks, CA: Sage.

Foster, Hal. 1983. "Postmodernism: A Preface." Pp. ix–xvi in H. Foster (ed.), *The Anti-Esthetic: Essays on Postmodern Culture*. Seattle: Bay Press.

Foucault, Michel. 1980. *Power/Knowledge: Selected Interviews and Other Writings, 1972–1977*. New York: Pantheon.

Foucault, Michel. 1978. *Discipline and Punish: The Birth of the Prison*. New York: Pantheon.

Frank, Thomas. 1997. *The Conquest of Cool: Business Culture, Counterculture, and the Rise of Hip Consumerism*. Chicago: University of Chicago Press.

Frankenberg, Ruth. 1993. *White Women, Race Matters: The Social Construction of Whiteness*. Minneapolis: University of Minnesota Press.

Frankenberg, Ruth (ed.). 1997. *Displacing Whiteness: Essays in Social and Cultural Criticism.* Durham, NC: Duke University Press.

Fraser, Nancy. 1995. "Politics, Culture, and the Public Sphere: Toward a Postmodern Conception." Pp. 287–312 in L. Nicholson and S. Seidman (eds.), *Social Postmodernism: Beyond Identity Politics.* Cambridge: Cambridge University Press.

Fraser, Nancy. 1992. "Rethinking the Public Sphere: A Contribution to the Critique of Actually Existing Democracy." Pp. 109–142 in C. Calhoun (ed.), *Habermas and the Public Sphere.* Cambridge: The MIT Press.

Gallop, Jane (ed.). 1995. *Pedagogy: The Question of Impersonation.* Bloomington: Indiana University Press.

Gardner, Carol Brooks. 1995. *Passing By: Gender and Public Harassment.* Berkeley: University of California Press.

Garoian, Charles. 1999. *Performing Pedagogy: Toward an Art of Politics.* Albany: State University of New York Press.

Geertz, Clifford. 1996. "Afterward." Pp. 259–262 in S. Feld and K. Basso (eds.), *Senses of Place.* New York: School of American Research Press.

Geertz, Clifford. 1973. *The Interpretation of Cultures.* New York: Basic Books.

Gieryn, Tom. 1994 "Objectivity for These Times." *Perspectives on Science* 2(3):324–349.

Gillespie, Marie. 1995. *Television, Ethnicity, and Cultural Change.* New York: Routledge.

Gilroy, Paul. 2000. "The Sugar You Stir." Pp. 126–133 in P. Gilroy, L. Grossberg, and A. McRobbie (eds.), *Without Guarantees: In Honour of Stuart Hall.* London: Verso.

Gilroy, Paul. 1993. *The Black Atlantic: Modernity and Double Consciousness.* Cambridge: Harvard University Press.

Giroux, Henry. 2003. *Public Spaces, Private Lives: Democracy Beyond 9/11.* Lanham, MD: Rowman and Littlefield.

Giroux, Henry. 2000. *Impure Acts: The Practical Politics of Cultural Studies.* New York: Routledge.

Giroux, Henry. 1996. *Fugitive Cultures: Race, Violence, and Youth.* New York: Routledge.

Giroux, Henry. 1994. *Disturbing Pleasures: Learning Popular Culture.* New York: Routledge.

Giroux, Henry 1993. "Literacy and the Politics of Difference." Pp. 367–377 in C. Lankshear and P. McLaren (eds.), *Critical Literacy: Politics, Praxis, and the Postmodern.* Albany: State University of New York Press.

Giroux, Henry. 1992. *Border Crossings: Cultural Workers and the Politics of Education.* New York: Routledge.

Giroux, Henry, and Peter McLaren. 1994. *Between Borders: Pedagogy and the Politics of Cultural Studies.* New York: Routledge.

Goldfarb, Brian. 2002. *Visual Pedagogy: Media Cultures in and Beyond the Classroom.* Durham, NC: Duke University Press.

Gordon, Avery. 1997. *Ghostly Matters: Haunting and the Sociological Imagination.* Minneapolis: University of Minnesota Press.

Gordon, Avery, and Christopher Newfield (eds.). 1996. *Mapping Multicultural-ism*. Minneapolis: University of Minnesota Press.

Gramsci, Antonio. 1971. *Selections from the Prison Notebooks*. New York: International Publishers.

Grossberg, Lawrence. 1997a. *Bringing it All Back Home: Essays on Cultural Studies*. Durham: Duke University Press.

Grossberg, Lawrence. 1997b. *Dancing in Spite of Myself: Essays on Popular Culture*. Durham: Duke University Press.

Grossberg, Lawrence. 1996. "Toward a Genealogy of the State of Cultural Studies." Pp. 131–147 in C. Nelson and D. Gaonkar (eds.), *Disciplinarity and Dissent in Cultural Studies*. New York: Routledge.

Grossberg, Lawrence. 1994. "Bringing it All Back Home: Pedagogy and Cultural Studies." Pp. 1–25 in H. Giroux and P. McLaren (eds.), *Between Borders: Pedagogy and the Politics of Cultural Studies*. New York: Routledge.

Grossberg, Lawrence. 1992. *We Gotta Get Out of This Place: Popular Conservatism and Postmodern Culture*. New York: Routledge.

Habermas, Jurgen. 1989/1962. *The Structural Transformation of the Public Sphere: An Inquiry into a Category of Bourgeois Society*. Cambridge: The MIT Press.

Hall, Stuart (edited by Lawrence Grossberg). 1996. "On Postmodernism and Articulation: An Interview with Stuart Hall." Pp. 131–150 in D. Morley and K-H Chen (eds.), *Stuart Hall: Critical Dialogues in Cultural Studies*. New York: Routledge.

Hall, Stuart. 1992. "What Is This 'Black' in Black Popular Culture?" Pp. 21–33 in G. Dent (ed.), *Black Popular Culture*. Seattle: Bay Press.

Hall, Stuart. 1980. "Encoding/Decoding." Pp. 128–138 in S. Hall, A. Lowe, and P. Willis (eds.), *Culture, Media, Language*. London: Hutchinson.

Haraway, Donna. 1991. *Simians, Cyborgs, and Women: The Reinvention of Nature*. New York: Routledge.

Haraway, Donna. 1990. "A Manifesto for Cyborgs: Science, Technology, and Socialist Feminism in the 1980s." Pp. 190–233 in L. Nicholson (ed.), *Feminism/Postmodernism*. New York: Routledge.

Hartley, Heather. 1999. "What's My Orientation? Using the Teacher-as-Text Strategy as Feminist Pedagogical Practice." *Teaching Sociology* 27(4):398–406.

Harvey, David. 1990. *The Condition of Postmodernity*. Cambridge, MA: Blackwell.

Hazen, Don, and Julie Winokur (eds.). 1997. *We the Media: A Citizens' Guide to Fighting for Media Democracy*. New York: The New Press.

Heath, Shirley Brice. 1983. *Ways With Words: Language, Life, and Work in Communities and Classrooms*. Cambridge: Cambridge University Press.

Hebdige, Dick. 1996. "Postmodernism and 'the Other side.'" Pp. 174–200 in D. Morley and K-H Chen (eds.), *Stuart Hall: Critical Dialogues in Cultural Studies*. New York: Routledge.

Hennessy, Rosemary. 1995. "Queer Visibility in Commodity Culture." Pp. 142–183 in L. Nicholson and S. Seidman (eds.), *Social Postmodernism: Beyond Identity Politics*. Cambridge: Cambridge University Press.

Hill, Mike. 2004. *After Whiteness: Unmaking an American Majority*. New York: New York University Press.

Hill, Mike (ed.). 1997. *Whiteness: A Critical Reader.* New York: New York University Press.

hooks, bell. 2003. *Teaching Community: A Pedagogy of Hope.* New York: Routledge.

hooks, bell. 1995. *Killing Rage: Ending Racism.* New York: Henry Holt.

hooks, bell. 1994a. *Teaching to Transgress: Education as the Practice of Freedom.* New York: Routledge.

hooks, bell. 1994b. *Outlaw Culture: Resisting Representations.* New York: Routledge.

hooks, bell. 1990. *Yearning: Race, Gender, and Cultural Politics.* Boston: South End Press.

Hudlin, Reginald, and Warrington Hudlin (producers). 1994. *Space Traders,* in *Cosmic Slop* (video recording). New York: Home Box Office.

Jacobs, Walter R. 2002. "Using Lower-Division Developmental Education Students as Teaching Assistants." *Research and Teaching in Developmental Education* 19(1):41–48.

Jacobs, Walter R. 1998. "The Teacher as Text: Using Personal Experience to Stimulate the Sociological Imagination." *Teaching Sociology* 26(3):222–228.

Jacobs, Walter R. 1997. "The Tide of Second-Wave Whiteness." *Symploke* 5(1–2):232–235.

Jacobs, Walter R., and Dwight E. Brooks. 1999. "Using Strange Texts to Teach Race, Ethnicity, and the Media." *The Velvet Light Trap* 44(Fall):31–38.

Jameson, Fredric. 1983. "Postmodernism and Consumer Society." Pp. 111–125 in H. Foster (ed.), *The Anti-Esthetic: Essays on Postmodern Culture.* Seattle: Bay Press.

Janesick, Valerie. 1994. "The Dance of Qualitative Research Design: Metaphor, Methodolatry, and Meaning." Pp. 209–219 in N. Denzin and Y. Lincoln (eds.), *Handbook of Qualitative Research.* Thousand Oaks, CA: Sage.

Johnson, Cheryl. 1995. "Disinfecting Dialogues." Pp.129–137 in J. Gallop (ed.), *Pedagogy: The Question of Impersonation.* Bloomington: Indiana University Press.

Kellner, Douglas. 2003. *Media Spectacle.* New York: Routledge.

Kellner, Douglas. 1999. "*The X-Files* and the Aesthetics and Politics of Postmodern Pop." *The Journal of Aesthetics and Art Criticism* 57(2):161–175.

Kellner, Douglas. 1995a. *Media Culture: Cultural Studies, Identity, and Politics between the Modern and the Postmodern.* New York: Routledge.

Kellner, Douglas. 1995b. "Cultural Studies, Multiculturalism, and Media Culture." Pp. 5–17 in G. Dines and J. Humez (eds.), *Gender, Race, and Class in Media.* Thousand Oaks, CA: Sage.

Kim, Elaine. 1993. "Home Is Where the *Han* Is: A Korean-American Perspective on the Los Angeles Upheavals." Pp. 215–235 in R. Gooding-Williams (ed.), *Reading Rodney King, Reading Urban Uprising.* New York: Routledge.

Kolodny, Annette. 1998. *Failing the Future: A Dean Looks at Higher Education in the Twenty-first Century.* Durham, NC: Duke University Press.

Kumar, Amitava (ed.). 1997. *Class Issues: Pedagogy, Cultural Studies, and the Public Sphere.* New York: New York University Press.

Kumashiro, Kevin. 2001. "'Posts' Perspectives on Anti-Oppressive Education in Social Studies, English, Mathematics, and Science Classrooms." *Educational Researcher* 30(3):3–12.

LaCapra, Dominick. 1997. "From What Subject-Position(s) Should One Address the Politics of Research?" Pp. 46–58 in E. Kaplan and G. Levine (eds.), *The Politics of Research*. New Brunswick, NJ: Rutgers University Press.

Lankshear, Colin, and Peter McLaren (eds.). 1993. *Critical Literacy: Politics, Praxis, and the Postmodern*. Albany: State University of New York Press.

Lee, Amy. 2000. *Composing Critical Pedagogies: Teaching Writing as Revision*. Urbana, IL: National Council of Teachers of Education.

Lemert, Charles. 1997. *Postmodernism Is Not What You Think*. Malden, MA: Blackwell.

Lightman, Alan. 1993. *Einstein's Dreams: A Novel*. New York: Pantheon.

Long, Gary, and Elise Lake. 1996. "A Precondition for Ethical Teaching: Clarity About Role and Inequality." *Teaching Sociology* 24:111–116.

Lubiano, Wahneema. 1996. "Like Being Mugged by a Metaphor: Multiculturalism and State Narratives." Pp. 64–75 in A. Gordon and C. Newfield (eds.), *Mapping Multiculturalism*. Minneapolis: University of Minnesota Press.

Lury, Celia. 1996. *Consumer Culture*. New Brunswick, NJ: Rutgers University Press.

Marcus, George. 1994. "What Comes (Just) After 'Post'?" Pp. 563–574 in N. Denzin and Y. Lincoln, *Handbook of Qualitative Research*. Thousand Oaks, CA: Sage.

Martin, Darnell (screenwriter and director). 1994. *I Like it Like That* (video recording). Los Angeles: Columbia Pictures.

McIntosh, Peggy. 1998. "White Privilege and Male Privilege: A Personal Account of Coming to See Correspondences Through Work in Women's Studies." Pp 94–105 in M. Anderson and P. Collins (eds.), *Race, Class, and Gender: An Anthology*, 3rd ed. New York: Wadsworth.

McLaren, Peter. 1995. *Critical Pedagogy and Predatory Culture: Oppositional Politics in a Postmodern Era*. New York: Routledge.

McLaren, Peter, and Colin Lankshear. 1993. "Critical Literacy and the Postmodern Turn." Pp. 379–419 in C. Lankshear and P. McLaren (eds.), *Critical Literacy: Politics, Praxis, and the Postmodern*. Albany: State University of New York Press.

McLaughlin, Thomas. 1996. *Street Smarts and Critical Literacy: Listening to the Vernacular*. Madison: University of Wisconsin Press.

Merton, Robert. 1973. *The Sociology of Science: Theoretical and Empirical Investigations*. Chicago: University of Chicago Press.

Miller, Laura. 1995. "Women and Children First: Gender and the Settling of the Electronic Frontier." Pp. 49–57 in J. Brook and I. Boal (eds.), *Resisting the Virtual Life*. San Francisco: City Lights Books.

Miller, Toby. 1998. *Technologies of Truth: Cultural Citizenship and the Popular Media*. Minneapolis: University of Minnesota Press.

Mills, C. Wright. 1959. *The Sociological Imagination*. London: Oxford University Press.

Moore, Melanie. 1997. "Student Resistance to Course Content: Reactions to the Gender of the Messenger." *Teaching Sociology* 25:128–33.

Morley, David, and Kuan-Hsing Chen (eds.). 1996. *Stuart Hall: Critical Dialogues in Cultural Studies*. New York: Routledge.

Morrison, Toni. 1992. *Playing in the Dark: Whiteness and the Literary Imagination*. Cambridge: Harvard University Press.

Mouffe, Chantal. 1995. "Feminism, Citizenship, and Radical Democratic Politics." Pp. 315–331 in L. Nicholson and S. Seidman (eds.), *Social Postmodernism: Beyond Identity Politics*. Cambridge: Cambridge University Press.

Nelson, Cary. 1997a. *Manifesto of a Tenured Radical*. New York: New York University Press.

Nelson, Cary (ed.). 1997b. *Will Eat For Food: Academic Labor in Crisis*. Minneapolis: University of Minnesota Press.

Neumann, Mark. 1996. "Collecting Ourselves at the End of the Century." Pp. 172–198 in C. Ellis and A. Bochner (eds.), *Composing Ethnography: Alternative Forms of Qualitative Writing*. Walnut Creek, CA: AltaMira Press.

Nicholson, Linda (ed.). 1990. *Feminism/Postmodernism*. New York: Routledge.

Nicholson, Linda and Steven Seidman (eds.). 1995. *Social Postmodernism: Beyond Identity Politics*. Cambridge: Cambridge University Press.

Oakes, J. Michael. 2002. "Risks and Wrongs in Social Science Research: An Evaluator's Guide to the IRB." *Evaluation Review* 24:443–478.

O'Brien, Judy, and Judith Howard. 1996. "To Be or Not to Be: The Paradox of Value-Neutrality and Responsible Authority." *Teaching Sociology* 24:326–330.

Omi, Michael, and Howard Winant. 1994. *Racial Formation in the United States*, 2nd ed. New York: Routledge.

O'Shea, Alan. 1998. "A Special Relationship? Cultural Studies, Academia, and Pedagogy." *Cultural Studies* 12(4):513–527.

Pedelty, Mark. 2001. "Stigma." Pp. 53–70 in J. Higbee (ed.), *2001: A Developmental Odyssey*. Warrensburg, MO: National Association for Developmental Education.

Phelan, Shane. 1995. "The Space of Justice: Lesbians and Democratic Politics." Pp. 332–356 in L. Nicholson and S. Seidman (eds.), *Social Postmodernism: Beyond Identity Politics*. Cambridge: Cambridge University Press.

Prashad, Vijay. 1997. "Other Worlds in a Fordist Classroom." Pp. 247–255 in A. Kumar (ed.), *Class Issues: Pedagogy, Cultural Studies, and the Public Sphere*. New York: New York University Press.

Richardson, Laurel. 1993. "Poetics, Dramatics, and Transgressive Validity: The Case of the Skipped Line." *The Sociological Quarterly* 34(4):695–710.

Robbins, Bruce. 1993. *The Phantom Public Sphere*. Minneapolis: University of Minnesota Press.

Ronai, Carol Rambo. 1994. "The Reflexive Self Through Narrative: A Night in the Life of an Erotic Dancer." Pp. 102–124 in C. Ellis and M. Flaherty (eds.), *Investigating Subjectivity: Research on Lived Experience*. Newbury Park, CA: Sage.

Rose, Tricia. 1994. *Black Noise: Rap Music and Black Culture in Contemporary America*. Hanover: Wesleyan University Press.

Rosenau, Pauline. 1993. *Post-Modernism and the Social Sciences: Insights, Inroads, and Intrusions*. Princeton: Princeton University Press.

Ross, Andrew. 1999. *The Celebration Chronicles: Life, Liberty, and the Pursuit of Property Value in Disney's New Town*. New York: Ballantine.

Rowling, J. K. 2000. *Harry Potter and the Goblet of Fire*. New York: Scholastic.

Sandell, Jillian. 1997. "Telling Stories of 'Queer White Trash'." Pp. 211–230 in M. Wray and A. Newitz (eds.), *White Trash: Race and Class in America*. New York: Routledge.

Schutz, Aaron. 2004. "Rethinking Domination and Resistance: Challenging Postmodernism." *Educational Researcher* 33(1):15–23.

Seidler, Victor. 1989. *Rediscovering Masculinity: Reason, Language, and Sexuality*. New York: Routledge.

Seidman, Steven. 1995. "Deconstructing Queer Theory, or the Under-Theorization of the Social and the Ethical." Pp. 116–141 in L. Nicholson and S. Seidman (eds.), *Social Postmodernism: Beyond Identity Politics*. Cambridge: Cambridge University Press.

Shaviro, Steven. 2003. *Connected: Or What it Means to Live in the Network Society*. Minneapolis: University of Minnesota Press.

Shepperd, Jerry. 1997. "Relevance and Responsibility: A Postmodern Response. Response to 'A Postmodern Explanation of Student Consumerism in Higher Education.'" *Teaching Sociology* 25:333–335.

Sholle, David, and Stan Denski. 1993. "Reading and Writing the Media: Critical Media Literacy and Postmodernism." Pp. 297–321 in C. Lankshear and P. McLaren (eds.), *Critical Literacy: Politics, Praxis, and the Postmodern*. Albany: State University of New York Press.

Simon, Roger. 1995. "Face to Face with Alterity." Pp. 90–105 in J. Gallop (ed.), *Pedagogy: The Question of Impersonation*. Bloomington: Indiana University Press.

Slack, Jennifer. 1996. "The Theory and Method of Articulation in Cultural Studies." Pp. 112–127 in D. Morley and K-H Chen (eds.), *Stuart Hall: Critical Dialogues in Cultural Studies*. New York: Routledge.

Spry, Tami. 2001. "Performing Autoethnography: An Embodied Methodological Praxis." *Qualitative Inquiry* 7(6):706–732.

Stabile, Carol. 1997. "Pedagogues, Pedagogy, and Political Struggle." Pp. 208–220 in A. Kumar (ed.), *Class Issues: Pedagogy, Cultural Studies, and the Public Sphere*. New York: New York University Press.

Steele, Shelby. 1990. *The Content of Our Character: A New Vision of Race in America*. New York: St. Martin's Press.

Sweet, Stephen. 1998a. "Practicing Radical Pedagogy: Balancing Ideals with Institutional Constraints." *Teaching Sociology* 26(2):100–111.

Sweet, Stephen. 1998b. "Reassessing Radical Pedagogy" *Teaching Sociology* 26(2):127–129.

Takata, Susan. 1997. "The Chairs Game—Competition Versus Cooperation: The Sociological Uses of Musical Chairs." *Teaching Sociology* 25:200–206.

Tannen, Deborah. 1990. *You Just Don't Understand: Women and Men in Conversation*. New York: Ballantine.

Trombley, Guy. 2001. "Interactive Class Websites as Research Tools: Student-Driven Meta-Analysis and Evaluation of Students' Learning Process." Paper presented at "Classrooms of the Future" conference (Minneapolis, May 23).

Tucker, Robert (ed.). 1978. *The Marx-Engels Reader*, 2nd ed. New York: Norton.

Turner, Graeme. 1996. *British Cultural Studies: An Introduction*, 2nd ed. New York: Routledge.

Tyler, Stephen. 1986. "Post-Modern Ethnography: From Document of the Occult to Occult Document." Pp. 122–140 in J. Clifford and G. Marcus (eds.), *Writing Culture: The Poetics and Politics of Ethnography*. Berkeley: University of California Press.

Vanderbilt, Tom. 1998. *The Sneaker Book: Anatomy of an Industry and an Icon*. New York: The New Press.

Van Maanen, John. 1988. *Tales of the Field: On Writing Ethnography*. Chicago: University of Chicago Press.

Visweswaran, Kamala. 1994. *Fictions of Feminist Ethnography*. Minneapolis: University of Minnesota Press.

Wald, Alan. 1997. "A Pedagogy of Unlearning." Pp. 125–147 in A. Kumar (ed.), *Class Issues: Pedagogy, Cultural Studies, and the Public Sphere*. New York: New York University Press.

Wallace, Michele. 1990. *Invisibility Blues: From Pop to Theory*. New York: Verso.

Warner, Michael (ed.). 1993. *Fear of a Queer Planet: Queer Politics and Social Theory*. Minneapolis: University of Minnesota Press.

Watson, Graham. 1987. "Make Me Reflexive—But Not Yet: Strategies for Managing Essential Reflexivity in Ethnographic Discourse." *Journal of Anthropological Research* 43(1):29–41.

Weintraub, Jeff, and Krishan Kumar. 1997. *Public and Private in Thought and Practice: Perspectives on a Grand Dichotomy*. Chicago: University of Chicago Press.

West, Cornel. 1990. "The New Cultural Politics of Difference." Pp. 19–36 in R. Ferguson, M. Gever, T.T. Minh-ha, and C. West (eds.), *Out There: Marginalization and Contemporary Cultures*. New York: The New Museum of Contemporary Art.

Williams, Emlyn (ed.). 1978. *Saki: Short Stories I*. London: J. M. Dent.

Woolgar, Steve. 1988. "Reflexivity Is the Ethnographer of the Text." Pp. 14–36 in S. Woolgar (ed.), *Knowledge and Reflexivity: New Frontiers in the Sociology of Knowledge*. Newbury Park, CA: Sage.

Wray, Matt, and Annalee Newitz (eds.). 1997. *White Trash: Race and Class in America*. New York: Routledge.

Index